SAM SHEPARD

Buried Child

Sam Shepard is the author of more than forty-five plays. He won the Pulitzer Prize for *Buried Child*. He was a finalist for the W. H. Smith Literary Award for his story collection *Great Dream of Heaven*, and he has also written the story collection *Cruising Paradise*, two collections of prose pieces, *Motel Chronicles* and *Hawk Moon*, and *Rolling Thunder Logbook*, a diary of Bob Dylan's 1975 Rolling Thunder Review tour. As an actor he has appeared in more than thirty films, including *Days of Heaven*, *Crimes of the Heart*, *Steel Magnolias*, *The Pelican Brief*, *Snow Falling on Cedars*, *All the Pretty Horses*, *Black Hawk Down*, and *The Notebook*. He received an Oscar nomination in 1984 for his performance in *The Right Stuff*. His screenplay for *Paris, Texas* won the Grand Jury Prize at the 1984 Cannes Film Festival, and he wrote and directed the film *Far North* in 1988 and cowrote and starred in Wim Wenders' *Don't Come Knocking* in 2005. Shepard's plays, eleven of which have won Obie Awards, include *The God of Hell*, *The Late Henry Moss*, *Simpatico*, *Curse of the Starving Class*, *True West*, *Fool for Love*, and *A Lie of the Mind*, which won a New York Drama Desk Award. A member of the American Academy of Arts and Letters, Shepard received the Gold Medal for Drama from the Academy in 1992, and in 1994 he was inducted into the Theatre Hall of Fame. He lives in New York.

SAM SHEPARD

Buried Child

A PLAY

Revised Edition

VINTAGE BOOKS

A Division of Random House, Inc.

New York

A VINTAGE ORIGINAL, FEBRUARY 2006

Originally published in the United States in the collection
Buried Child, Seduced, & Suicide in B♭ by Urizen Books, Inc., New York, in
1979. Revised in 1997 by Dramatists Play Service, Inc., New York.

Library of Congress Cataloging-in-Publication Data
Shepard, Sam, 1943–
Buried child : a play / Sam Shepard.—Rev. ed.
p. cm.
1. Farm life—Drama. 2. Family—Drama. I. Title.
PS3569.H394 B87 2006
812'.54—dc22
2005054691

Vintage ISBN-10: 0-307-27497-7
Vintage ISBN-13: 978-0-307-27497-7

Book design by Rebecca Aidlin

www.vintagebooks.com

Printed in the United States of America
10 9

For Joe Chaikin

PREFACE TO THE
REVISED EDITION

In 1978, when we first produced *Buried Child* at the Magic Theatre in San Francisco, I had an uneasy feeling about it. Although I was more than satisfied with the production, the actors, the set, etc., aspects of the writing still seemed awkward and unfinished. The Pulitzer Prize did not change my opinion in this regard, but by that time I was already on to other work and had no inclination to double back. When Gary Sinise started work on the Steppenwolf production in Chicago in 1995, enough time had elapsed for me to clearly see the holes in the play. This insight was also heightened by Gary's instinct to push the characters and situation into an almost burlesque territory, which seemed suddenly right. It became clear, for instance, that Halie's offstage voice in the opening scene went on too long and that Lois Smith (playing the part) was bringing a sharp irony and wit to it that deserved special attention. The sexual innuendos between Dodge (James Gammon) and Shelly (Kellie Overbey) needed to be more overt and less coy. But, most important, the character of Vince seemed to be hanging in the wind, without real purpose. Even though a core truth of this character is his aimlessness and passivity, there seemed to be no point in allowing him to be completely outside the play almost in the predicament of a narrator. So I began to try to find ways to bring him around, to "see the light," as it were, without turning him into some kind of hero or even Sherlock Holmes. Finally, the language began to settle in and take hold. There were fewer gaps between the actors, the characters, and the words. I'm very grateful for having had the opportunity to do this work. It's now a better play.

Sam Shepard
July 2005

Buried Child

Buried Child, the revised edition, was produced on Broadway at the Brooks Atkinson Theatre by Frederick Zollo, Nicholas Paleologos, Jane Harmon, Nina Keneally, Gary Sinise, Edwin Schloss, and Liz Oliver on April 30, 1996. The production transferred from the premiere production at Steppenwolf Theatre Company (Martha Lavey, Artistic Director; Michael Gennaro, Managing Director) in Chicago, Illinois, which opened on October 1, 1995. It was directed by Gary Sinise; the set design was by Robert Brill; the costume design was by Allison Reeds; the lighting design was by Kevin Rigdon; the sound design was by Rob Milburn; and the production stage manager was Laura Koch. The cast was as follows:

DODGE	James Gammon
HALIE	Lois Smith
TILDEN	Terry Kinney
BRADLEY	Leo Burmester
SHELLY	Kellie Overbey
VINCE	Jim True
FATHER DEWIS	Jim Mohr

Buried Child was produced at Theater for the New City, in New York City, on October 19, 1978. It was directed by Robert Woodruff. The cast was as follows:

DODGE	Richard Hamilton
HALIE	Jacqueline Brookes
TILDEN	Tom Noonan
BRADLEY	Jay O. Sanders
SHELLY	Mary McDonnell
VINCE	Christopher McCann
FATHER DEWIS	Bill Wiley

Buried Child received its premiere at the Magic Theatre, in San Francisco, California, on June 27, 1978. It was directed by Robert Woodruff. The cast was as follows:

DODGE	Joseph Gistirak
HALIE	Catherine Willis
TILDEN	Dennis Ludlow
BRADLEY	William M. Carr
SHELLY	Betsy Scott
VINCE	Barry Lane
FATHER DEWIS	Rj Frank

CHARACTERS

DODGE	in his seventies
HALIE	Dodge's wife; mid-sixties
TILDEN	their oldest son
BRADLEY	their next oldest son, an amputee
VINCE	Tilden's son
SHELLY	Vince's girlfriend
FATHER DEWIS	a Protestant minister

Act One

Scene: day. Old wooden staircase down left with pale, frayed carpet laid down on the steps. The stairs lead offstage left up into the wings with no landing. Up right is an old, dark green sofa with the stuffing coming out in spots. Stage right of the sofa is an upright lamp with a faded yellow shade and a small night table with several small bottles of pills on it. Down right of the sofa, with the screen facing the sofa, is a large, old-fashioned brown TV. A flickering blue light comes from the screen, but no image, no sound. In the dark, the light of the lamp and the TV slowly brighten in the black space. The space behind the sofa, upstage, is a large screened-in porch with a board floor. A solid interior door to stage right of the sofa leads from the porch to the outside. Beyond that are the shapes of dark elm trees.

Gradually the form of DODGE *is made out, sitting on the couch, facing the TV, the blue light flickering on his face. He wears a well-worn T-shirt, suspenders, khaki work pants, and brown slippers. He's covered himself in an old brown blanket. He's very thin and sickly looking, in his late seventies. He just stares at the TV. More light fills the stage softly. The sound of light rain.* DODGE *slowly tilts his head back and stares at the ceiling for a while, listening to the rain. He lowers his head again and stares at the TV. He starts to cough slowly and softly.*

The coughing gradually builds. He holds one hand to his mouth and tries to stifle it. The coughing gets louder, then suddenly stops when he hears the sound of his wife's voice coming from the top of the staircase.

HALIE'S VOICE: Dodge? (DODGE *just stares at the TV. Long pause. He stifles two short coughs.*) Dodge! You want a pill, Dodge? (*He doesn't answer. Takes a bottle out from under a cushion of the sofa and takes a long swig. Puts the bottle back, stares at the TV, pulls the blanket up around his neck.*) You know what it is, don't you? It's the rain! Weather. That's it. Every time. Every time you get like this, it's the rain. No sooner does the rain start than you start. (*Pause.*) Dodge? (*He makes no reply. Pulls a pack of cigarettes out from his sweater and lights one. Stares at the TV. Pause.*) You should see it coming down up here. Just coming down in sheets. Blue sheets. The bridge is pretty near flooded. What's it like down there? Dodge? (DODGE *turns his head back over his left shoulder and takes a look out through the porch. He turns back to the TV.*)

DODGE: (*To himself.*) Catastrophic.

HALIE'S VOICE: What? What'd you say, Dodge?

DODGE: (*Louder.*) It looks like rain to me! Plain old rain!

HALIE'S VOICE: Rain? Of course it's rain! Are you having a seizure or something! Dodge? (*Pause.*) I'm coming down there in about five minutes if you don't answer me!

DODGE: Don't come down.

HALIE'S VOICE: What!

DODGE: (*Louder.*) Don't come down! (*He has another coughing attack. Stops.*)

HALIE'S VOICE: You should take a pill for that! I don't see why you just don't take a pill. Be done with it once and for all. Put a stop to it. (*He takes the bottle out again. Another swig. Returns the bottle.*) It's not Christian, but it works. It's not necessarily Christian, that is. A pill. We don't know. We're not in a position to answer something like that. There's some things the ministers can't even answer. I, personally, can't see anything wrong with it. A pill. Pain is pain. Pure and simple. Suffering is a different matter. That's entirely different. A pill seems as good an answer as any. Dodge? (*Pause.*) Dodge, are you watching baseball?

DODGE: No.

HALIE'S VOICE: What?

DODGE: (*Louder.*) No! I'm *not* watching baseball.

HALIE'S VOICE: What're you watching? You shouldn't be watching anything that'll get you excited!

DODGE: Nothing gets me excited.

HALIE'S VOICE: No horse racing!

DODGE: They don't race here on Sundays.

HALIE'S VOICE: What?

DODGE: (*Louder.*) They don't race on Sundays!

HALIE'S VOICE: Well, they shouldn't race on Sundays. The Sabbath.

DODGE: Well, they don't! Not here anyway. The boondocks.

HALIE'S VOICE: Good. I'm amazed they still have that kind of legislation. Some semblance of morality. That's amazing.

DODGE: Yeah, it's amazing.

HALIE'S VOICE: What?

DODGE: (*Louder.*) It *is* amazing!

HALIE'S VOICE: It is. It truly is. I would've thought these days they'd be racing on Christmas even. A big flashing Christmas tree right down at the finish line.

DODGE: (*Shakes his head.*) No. Not yet.

HALIE'S VOICE: They used to race on New Year's! I remember that.

DODGE: They never raced on New Year's!

HALIE'S VOICE: Sometimes they did.

DODGE: They never did!

HALIE'S VOICE: Before we were married they did!

DODGE: "Before we were married." (DODGE *waves his hand in disgust at the staircase. Leans back in sofa. Stares at TV.*)

HALIE'S VOICE: I went once. With a man. On New Year's.

DODGE: (*Mimicking her.*) Oh, a "man."

HALIE'S VOICE: What?

DODGE: Nothing!

HALIE'S VOICE: A wonderful man. A breeder.

DODGE: A what?

HALIE'S VOICE: A breeder! A horse breeder! Thoroughbreds.

DODGE: Oh, thoroughbreds. Wonderful. You betcha. A breeder-man.

HALIE'S VOICE: That's right. He knew everything there was to know.

DODGE: I bet he taught you a thing or two, huh? Gave you a good turn around the old stable!

HALIE'S VOICE: Knew everything there was to know about horses. We won bookoos of money that day.

DODGE: What?

HALIE'S VOICE: Money! We won every race I think.

DODGE: Bookoos?

HALIE'S VOICE: Every single race.

DODGE: Bookoos of money?

HALIE'S VOICE: It was one of those kind of days.

DODGE: New Year's!

HALIE'S VOICE: Yes! It might've been Florida. Or California! One of those two.

DODGE: Can I take my pick?

HALIE'S VOICE: It was Florida!

DODGE: Aha!

HALIE'S VOICE: Wonderful! Absolutely wonderful! The sun was just gleaming. Flamingos. Bougainvilleas. Palm trees.

DODGE: (*To himself, mimicking her.*) Flamingos. Bougainvilleas.

HALIE'S VOICE: Everything was dancing with life! Colors. There were all kinds of people from everywhere. Everyone was dressed to the nines. Not like today. Not like they dress today. People had a sense of style.

DODGE: When was this anyway?

HALIE'S VOICE: This was long before I knew you.

DODGE: Must've been.

HALIE'S VOICE: Long before. I was escorted.

DODGE: To Florida?

HALIE'S VOICE: Yes. Or it might've been California. I'm not sure which.

DODGE: All that way you were escorted?

HALIE'S VOICE: Yes.

DODGE: And he never laid a finger on you, I suppose? This gentleman breeder-man. (*Long silence.*) Halie? Are we still in the land of the living? (*No answer. Long pause.*)

HALIE'S VOICE: Are you going out today?

DODGE: (*Gesturing toward rain.*) In this?

HALIE'S VOICE: I'm just asking a simple question.

DODGE: I rarely go out in the bright sunshine, why would I go out in this?

HALIE'S VOICE: I'm just asking because I'm not doing any shopping today. And if you need anything you should ask Tilden.

DODGE: Tilden's not here!

HALIE'S VOICE: He's in the kitchen. (DODGE *looks toward left, then back toward the TV.*)

DODGE: All right.

HALIE'S VOICE: What?

DODGE: (*Louder.*) All right! I'll ask Tilden!

HALIE'S VOICE: Don't scream. It'll only get your coughing started.

DODGE: Scream? Men don't scream.

HALIE'S VOICE: Just tell Tilden what you want and he'll get it. (*Pause.*) Bradley should be over later.

DODGE: Bradley?

HALIE'S VOICE: Yes. To cut your hair.

DODGE: My hair? I don't need my hair cut! I haven't hardly got any hair left!

HALIE'S VOICE: It won't hurt!

DODGE: I don't need it!

HALIE'S VOICE: It's been more than two weeks, Dodge.

DODGE: I don't need it! And I never did need it!

HALIE'S VOICE: I have to meet Father Dewis for lunch.

DODGE: You tell Bradley that if he shows up here with those clippers, I'll separate him from his manhood!

HALIE'S VOICE: I won't be very late. No later than four at the very latest.

DODGE: You tell him! Last time he left me near bald! And I wasn't even awake!

HALIE'S VOICE: That's not my fault!

DODGE: You put him up to it!

HALIE'S VOICE: I never did!

DODGE: You did too! You had some fancy, idiot house-social planned! Time to dress up the corpse for company! Lower the ears a little! Put up a little front! Surprised you didn't tape a pipe to my mouth while you were at it! That woulda looked nice! Huh? A pipe? Maybe a bowler hat! Maybe a copy of the *Wall Street Journal* casually placed on my lap! A fat labrador retriever at my feet.

HALIE'S VOICE: You always imagine the worst things of people!

DODGE: That's the least of the worst!

HALIE'S VOICE: I don't need to hear it! All day long I hear things like that and I don't need to hear more.

DODGE: You better tell him!

HALIE'S VOICE: You tell him yourself! He's your own son. You should be able to talk to your own son.

DODGE: Not while I'm sleeping! He cut my hair while I was sleeping!

HALIE'S VOICE: Well he won't do it again.

DODGE: There's no guarantee. He's a snake, that one.

HALIE'S VOICE: I promise he won't do it without your consent.

DODGE: (*After pause.*) There's no reason for him to even come over here.

HALIE'S VOICE: He feels responsible.

DODGE: For my hair?

HALIE'S VOICE: For your appearance.

DODGE: My appearance is out of his domain! It's even out of mine! In fact, it's disappeared! I'm an invisible man!

HALIE'S VOICE: Don't be ridiculous.

DODGE: He better not try it. That's all I've got to say.

HALIE'S VOICE: Tilden will watch out for you.

DODGE: Tilden won't protect me from Bradley!

HALIE'S VOICE: Tilden's the oldest. He'll protect you.

DODGE: Tilden can't even protect himself!

HALIE'S VOICE: Not so loud! He'll hear you. He's right in the kitchen.

DODGE: (*Yelling off left.*) Tilden!

HALIE'S VOICE: Dodge, what are you trying to do?

DODGE: (*Yelling off left.*) Tilden, get your ass in here!

HALIE'S VOICE: Why do you enjoy stirring things up?

DODGE: I don't enjoy anything!

HALIE'S VOICE: That's a terrible thing to say.

DODGE: Tilden!

HALIE'S VOICE: That's the kind of statement that leads people right to an early grave.

DODGE: Tilden!

HALIE'S VOICE: It's no wonder people have turned their backs on Jesus!

DODGE: TILDEN!!

HALIE'S VOICE: It's no wonder the messengers of God's word are shouting louder now than ever before. Screaming to the four winds.

DODGE: TILDEN!!!! (DODGE *goes into a violent, spasmodic coughing attack as* TILDEN *enters from left, his arms loaded with fresh ears of corn.* TILDEN *is* DODGE's *oldest son, late forties, wears heavy construction boots covered with mud, dark green work pants, a plaid shirt, and a faded brown windbreaker. He has a butch haircut, wet from the rain. Something about him is profoundly burned-out and displaced. He stops center with the ears of corn in his arms and just stares at* DODGE *until he slowly finishes his coughing attack.* DODGE *looks up at him slowly.* DODGE *stares at the corn. Long pause as they watch each other.*)

HALIE'S VOICE: Dodge, if you don't take that pill nobody's going to force you. Least of all me. There's no honor in self-destruction. No honor at all. (*The two men ignore the voice.*)

DODGE: (*To* TILDEN.) Where'd you get that?

TILDEN: Picked it.

DODGE: You picked all that? (TILDEN *nods.*) Y~ company?

TILDEN: No.

DODGE: Where'd you pick it from?

TILDEN: Right out back.

DODGE: Out back where?!

TILDEN: Right out in back.

DODGE: There's nothing out there—in back.

TILDEN: There's corn.

DODGE: There hasn't been corn out there since about nineteen thirty-five! That's the last time I planted corn out there!

TILDEN: It's out there now.

The earth is bursting forth

DODGE: (*Yelling at stairs.*) Halie!

HALIE'S VOICE: Yes, dear! Have you come to your senses?

DODGE: Tilden's brought a whole bunch of sweet corn in here! There's no corn out back, is there?

TILDEN: (*To himself.*) There's tons of corn.

HALIE'S VOICE: Not that I know of!

DODGE: That's what I thought.

HALIE'S VOICE: Not since about nineteen thirty-five!

DODGE: (*To* TILDEN.) That's right. Nineteen thirty-five. That was the last of it.

TILDEN: It's out there now.

DODGE: You go and take that corn back to wherever you got it from!

TILDEN: (*After pause, staring at* DODGE.) It's picked. I picked it all in the rain. Once it's picked you can't put it back.

DODGE: I haven't had trouble with the neighbors here for fifty-seven years. I don't even know who the neighbors are! And I don't wanna know! Now go put that corn back where it came from! (TILDEN *stares at* DODGE, *then walks slowly over to him and dumps all the corn on* DODGE'S *lap and*

DODGE: I know you're not. I'm not worried about that. That's not the reason I brought it up.

TILDEN: What's the reason?

DODGE: The reason is I'm wondering what you're gonna do with yourself.

TILDEN: You're not worried about me, are you?

DODGE: I'm not worried about you. No. I'm just wondering.

TILDEN: You weren't worried about me when I wasn't here. When I was in New Mexico.

DODGE: No, I wasn't worried about you then either.

TILDEN: You shoulda worried about me then.

DODGE: Why's that? You didn't do anything down there, did you? Nothin' serious.

TILDEN: I didn't do anything. No.

DODGE: Then why should I have worried about you?

TILDEN: Because I was by myself.

DODGE: By yourself?

TILDEN: Yeah. I was by myself more than I've ever been before.

DODGE: Why was that? (*Pause.*)

TILDEN: Could I have some of that whiskey you've got?

DODGE: What whiskey? I haven't got any whiskey.

TILDEN: You've got some under the sofa.

DODGE: I haven't got anything under the sofa! Now mind your own damn business! Judas Priest, you come into the house outta the middle of nowhere, haven't heard or seen you in twenty-some years and suddenly you're making accusations.

TILDEN: I'm not making accusations.

DODGE: You're accusing me of hoarding whiskey under the sofa!

TILDEN: I'm not accusing you.

DODGE: You just got through telling me that I had whiskey under the sofa!

HALIE'S VOICE: Dodge?

DODGE: (*To* TILDEN.) Now she knows about it!

TILDEN: She doesn't know about it.

DODGE: She knows!

HALIE'S VOICE: Dodge, are you talking to yourself down there?

DODGE: I'm talking to Tilden!

HALIE'S VOICE: Tilden's down there?

DODGE: He's right here!

HALIE'S VOICE: What?

DODGE: (*Louder.*) He's right here!

HALIE'S VOICE: What's he doing?!

DODGE: (*To* TILDEN.) Don't answer her.

TILDEN: (*To* DODGE.) I'm not doing anything wrong.

DODGE: (*To* TILDEN.) I know you're not.

HALIE'S VOICE: What's he doing down there?

DODGE: (*To* TILDEN.) Don't answer. Whatever you do, don't answer her.

TILDEN: I'm not.

HALIE'S VOICE: Dodge! (*The men sit in silence.* DODGE *lights a cigarette.* TILDEN *keeps husking corn, spits tobacco now and then in the spittoon.*) Dodge! He's not drinking anything, is he? You see to it that he doesn't drink anything! You've gotta watch out for him. It's our responsibility. He can't look after himself anymore, so we have to do it. Nobody else will do it. We can't just send him away somewhere. If we had lots of money we could send him away. But we don't. We never will. That's why we have to stay healthy. You and me. Nobody's going to look after us. Bradley can't look after us. Bradley can hardly look after himself. I was always hoping that Tilden would look out for Bradley when they got older. After Bradley lost his leg. Tilden's the oldest. I always thought he'd be the one to take responsibility. I had no idea in the world that Tilden would be so much trouble. Who would've dreamed? Tilden was an All-American, don't forget. Don't forget that. Fullback. Or quarterback. I forget which.

TILDEN: (*To himself.*) Halfback.

DODGE: Don't make a peep. Just let her babble. (TILDEN *goes on husking.*)

HALIE'S VOICE: Then when Tilden turned out to be so much trouble, I put all my hopes on Ansel. Of course Ansel wasn't as handsome, but he was smart. He was the smartest probably. I think he probably was. Smarter than Bradley, that's for sure. Didn't go and chop his leg off with a chain saw. Smart enough not to go and do that. I think he was smarter than Tilden, too. Especially after Tilden got in all that trouble. Doesn't take brains to go to jail. Anybody knows that. 'Course then when Ansel passed, that left us all alone. Same as being alone. No different. Same as if they'd all died. He was the smartest. He could've earned lots of money. Lots and lots of money.

TILDEN: It's a mystery to me. I was out in back there. And the rain was coming down. And I didn't feel like coming back inside. I didn't feel the cold so much. I didn't mind the wet. So I was just walking. I was muddy but I didn't mind the mud so much. And I looked up. And I saw this stand of corn. In fact I was standing in it. Surrounded. It was over my head.

HALIE: There isn't any corn outside, Tilden! There's no corn! It's not the season for corn. Now, you must've either stolen this corn or you bought it.

DODGE: He doesn't have a red cent to his name. He's totally dependent.

HALIE: (*To* TILDEN.) So you stole it!

TILDEN: I didn't steal it. I don't want to get kicked out of Illinois. I was kicked out of New Mexico and I don't want to get kicked out of Illinois.

HALIE: You're going to get kicked out of this house, Tilden, if you don't tell me where you got that corn! (TILDEN *starts crying softly to himself but keeps husking corn. Pause.*)

DODGE: (*To* HALIE.) Why'd you have to tell him that? Who cares where he got the corn? Why'd you have to go and threaten him with expulsion?

HALIE: (*To* DODGE.) It's your fault, you know! You're the one that's behind all of this! I suppose you thought it'd be funny! Some joke! Cover the house with corn husks. You better get this cleaned up before Bradley sees it.

DODGE: Bradley's not getting in the front door!

HALIE: (*Kicking husks, striding back and forth.*) Bradley's going to be very upset when he sees this. He doesn't like to see the house in disarray. He can't stand it when one thing is out of place. The slightest thing. You know how he gets.

DODGE: Bradley doesn't even live here!

HALIE: It's his home as much as ours. He was born in this house!

DODGE: He was born in a hog wallow.

HALIE: Don't you say that! Don't you ever say that!

DODGE: He was born in a goddamn hog wallow! That's where he was born and that's where he belongs! He doesn't belong in this house! (HALIE *stops.*)

HALIE: I don't know what's come over you, Dodge. I don't know what in the world's come over you. You've become an evil, spiteful, vengeful man. You used to be a good man.

DODGE: Six of one, a half dozen of another.

HALIE: You sit here day and night, festering away! Decomposing! Smelling up the house with your putrid body!

Act Two

Scene: same set as Act One. Night. Sound of rain. DODGE *is still asleep on the sofa. His hair is cut extremely short and in places the scalp is cut and bleeding. His cap is still center stage. All the corn and husks, pail and milking stool have been cleared away. The lights come up to the sound of a young girl laughing offstage left.* DODGE *remains asleep.* SHELLY *and* VINCE *appear up left outside the screen porch door sharing the shelter of* VINCE's *overcoat above their heads.* SHELLY *is about nineteen, black hair, very beautiful. She wears tight jeans, high heels, a purple T-shirt, and a short rabbit fur coat. Her makeup is exaggerated and her hair has been curled.* VINCE *is* TILDEN's *son, about twenty-two. He wears a plaid shirt, jeans, dark glasses, and cowboy boots, and carries a black saxophone case. They shake the rain off themselves as they enter the porch through the screen door.*

SHELLY: (*Laughing, gesturing to the house.*) This is it? I don't believe this is it!

VINCE: This is it.

SHELLY: This is the house?

VINCE: This is the house.

SHELLY: I don't believe it!

VINCE: How come? It's just a house.

SHELLY: It's like a Norman Rockwell cover or something.

VINCE: What's a matter with that? It's American.

SHELLY: American? Where's the milkman and the little dog? What's the little dog's name? Spot. Spot and Jane. Dick and Jane and Spot. See Spot run.

VINCE: Come on! Knock it off. It's my heritage. (*She laughs more hysterically, out of control.*) Have some respect, would ya!

SHELLY: (*Trying to control herself.*) I'm sorry.

VINCE: I don't want to go in there with you acting like an idiot.

SHELLY: Yes, sir!

VINCE: Well, I don't. I haven't had any contact with them for years. I just don't want them to think I've suddenly arrived out of the middle of nowhere completely deranged.

SHELLY: What do you want them to think then? (*Pause.*)

VINCE: Nothing. Let's just go in. (*He crosses the porch toward right interior door.* SHELLY *follows him. He opens the right door slowly.* VINCE *sticks his head in, doesn't notice* DODGE *sleeping. Calls out toward staircase.*) Grandma! (SHELLY *breaks into laughter, unseen behind* VINCE. VINCE *pulls his head back outside and pulls the door shut. We hear their voices again without seeing them.*)

SHELLY: (*Stops laughing.*) I'm sorry. I'm sorry, Vince. I really am. I really am sorry. I won't do it again. I couldn't help it.

VINCE: It's not all that humorous.

SHELLY: I know it's not. I'm sorry.

VINCE: I mean this is a tense situation for me! I haven't seen them for over six years. I don't know what to expect.

SHELLY: I know. I won't do it again. Scout's honor. Just don't say "Grandma," okay? (*She giggles, stops.*) I mean if you say "Grandma," I don't know if I can control myself.

VINCE: Well, try!

SHELLY: Okay. Sorry. (*He opens the door again.* VINCE *sticks his head in, then enters.* SHELLY *follows behind him.* VINCE *crosses to the staircase, sets down the saxophone case and overcoat, looks up the staircase.* SHELLY *notices* DODGE's *baseball cap. Crosses to it. Picks it up and puts it on her head.* VINCE *goes up the stairs and disappears at the top.* SHELLY *watches him, then turns and sees* DODGE *on the sofa. She takes off the baseball cap.*)

VINCE: (*From upstairs.*) Grandma! (*From upstairs.*) Grandma! (SHELLY *crosses over to* DODGE *slowly and stands next to him. She stands at his head, reaches out slowly, and touches one of the cuts. The second she touches his head,* DODGE *jerks up to a sitting position on the sofa, eyes open.* SHELLY *gasps.* DODGE *looks at her, sees his cap in her hands, and quickly puts his hand to his bare head. He glares at* SHELLY, *then whips the cap out of her hands and puts it on.* SHELLY *backs away from him.* DODGE *stares at her.*)

SHELLY: I'm uh—with Vince. (DODGE *just glares at her.*) He's upstairs. (DODGE *looks at the staircase then back at* SHELLY. *Calling upstairs.*) Vince!

VINCE: Just a second!

SHELLY: You better get down here!

VINCE: Just a minute! I'm looking at the pictures. (DODGE *keeps staring at her.*)

SHELLY: (*To* DODGE.) We just got here. We drove out from New York. Pouring rain on the freeway so we thought we'd stop by. I mean Vince was planning on stopping anyway. He wanted to see you. He said he hadn't seen you in a long time. Pay you a little visit. (*Pause.* DODGE *just keeps staring at her.*) We were going all the way through to New Mexico. To see his father. I guess his father lives out there. In a trailer or something. (*Louder.*) We thought we'd stop by and see you on the way. Kill two birds with one stone, you know? (*She laughs.* DODGE *stares; she stops laughing.*) I

46

mean Vince has this thing about his family now. I guess it's a new thing with him. I kind of find it hard to relate to. But he feels it's important. You know. I mean he wants to get to know you again. After all this time. Reunite. I don't have much faith in it myself. Reuniting. (*Pause.* DODGE *just stares at her. She moves nervously to the staircase and yells up to* VINCE.) Vince, will you come down here please?! (VINCE *comes halfway down the stairs.*)

VINCE: I guess they went out for a while. (SHELLY *points to the sofa and* DODGE. VINCE *turns and sees* DODGE. *He comes all the way down the staircase and crosses to* DODGE. SHELLY *stays behind, near the staircase, keeping her distance.*) Grandpa? (DODGE *looks up at him, not recognizing him.*)

DODGE: Did you bring the whiskey? (VINCE *looks back at* SHELLY *then back to* DODGE.)

VINCE: Grandpa, it's me. Vince. I'm Vince. Tilden's son. You remember? (DODGE *stares at him.*)

DODGE: You didn't do what you told me. You didn't stay here with me.

VINCE: Grandpa, I haven't been here until just now. I just got here.

DODGE: You left. Abandoned me. You went outside like we told you not to do. You went out there in back. In the rain. (VINCE *looks back at* SHELLY. *She moves slowly toward the sofa.*)

SHELLY: Is he okay?

VINCE: I don't know. (*Takes off his shades.*) Look, Grandpa, don't you remember me? Vince. Your grandson. I know it's been a while. My hair's longer, maybe. (DODGE *stares at him, then takes off his baseball cap.*)

DODGE: (*Points to his head.*) See what happens when you leave me alone? See that? That's what happens. (VINCE *looks at* DODGE's *head, then reaches out to touch it.* DODGE *slaps* VINCE's *hand away with the cap and puts it back on his head.*)

VINCE: What's going on, Grandpa? Where's Halie?

DODGE: Don't worry about her. She won't be back for days. She's absconded. She says she'll be back but she won't be. (*He starts laughing.*) There's life in the old girl yet! (*Stops laughing.*)

VINCE: How did you do that to your head?

DODGE: I didn't do it! Don't be ridiculous! Whadya think I am, an animal?

VINCE: Well, who did then? (*Pause.* DODGE *stares at* VINCE.)

DODGE: Who do you think did it? Who do you think? (SHELLY *moves toward* VINCE.)

SHELLY: Vince, maybe we oughta go. I don't like this. I mean this isn't my idea of a good time.

VINCE: (*To* SHELLY.) Just a second. (*To* DODGE.) Grandpa, look, I just got here. I just now got here. I haven't been here for six years. I don't know anything that's happened. (*Pause.* DODGE *stares at him.*)

DODGE: You don't know anything?

VINCE: No.

DODGE: Well, that's good. That's good. It's much better not to know anything. Much, much better.

VINCE: Isn't there anybody here with you? (DODGE *turns slowly and looks off to left.*)

DODGE: Tilden's here.

VINCE: No, Grandpa, Tilden's in New Mexico. That's where I was going. I'm going out there to see him. We just stopped off here because it was on the way. (DODGE *turns slowly back to* VINCE.)

DODGE: Well, you're gonna be disappointed. (VINCE *backs away and joins* SHELLY. DODGE *stares at them.*)

SHELLY: Vince, why don't we spend the night in a motel and come back in the morning? We could have breakfast. A shower. Maybe everything would be different.

VINCE: Don't be scared. There's nothing to be scared of. He's just old.

SHELLY: I'm not scared!

DODGE: You two are not my idea of the perfect couple!

SHELLY: (*After pause.*) Oh really? Why's that?

VINCE: Shh! Don't aggravate him.

DODGE: There's something wrong between the two of you. Something not compatible. Like chalk and cheese.

VINCE: Grandpa, where did Halie go? Maybe we should call her. I don't understand why you're here all by yourself. Isn't anybody looking after you?

DODGE: What are you talking about? Do you know what you're talking about? Are you just talking for the sake of talking? Lubricating the gums?

VINCE: I'm just trying to—

DODGE: Halie is out with her boyfriend. The Right Reverend Dewis. He's not a breeder-man but a man of God. Next best thing, I suppose.

VINCE: I'm trying to figure out what's going on here!

DODGE: Good luck.

VINCE: I expected everything to be different. I mean the same. Like it used to be.

DODGE: Who are you to expect anything? Who are you supposed to be?

VINCE: I'm Vince! Your grandson! You've gotta remember me.

DODGE: Vince. My grandson. That's rich!

VINCE: Tilden's son.

DODGE: Tilden's son, Vince. He had *two*, I guess.

VINCE: Two? No look, you haven't seen me for a long time.

DODGE: When was the last time?

VINCE: I don't remember exactly. We had a big dinner. A reunion, kind of. Turkey. You made some comment about Dad's fastball. I was a kid, I guess. It was quite a while ago.

DODGE: You don't remember?

VINCE: No. Not really. I mean—we were all sitting at the table. All of us—and you and Bradley were making fun of Dad's fastball. And—

DODGE: You don't remember. How am I supposed to remember if you don't?

VINCE: I remember being there. I just don't remember the details.

SHELLY: Vince, come on. This isn't going to work out. I've got a strong feeling.

VINCE: (*To* SHELLY.) Just take it easy.

SHELLY: I'm taking it easy! He doesn't even know who you are!

VINCE: (*Crossing to* DODGE.) Of course he knows who I am. He's just tired or something. Grandpa, look—I don't know what's happened here, but—

DODGE: Stay where you are! Keep your distance! (VINCE *stops. Looks back at* SHELLY *then to* DODGE.)

SHELLY: Vince, this is really making me nervous. I mean he doesn't even want us here. He doesn't even like us.

DODGE: She's a beautiful girl.

VINCE: Thanks.

DODGE: Very "fetching," as they used to say.

SHELLY: Oh my God.

DODGE: (*To* SHELLY.) What's your name, girlie girl?

SHELLY: Shelly.

DODGE: Shelly. That's a man's name, isn't it?

SHELLY: Not in this case.

DODGE: (*To* VINCE.) She's a smart-ass too.

SHELLY: Vince! Can we go?

VINCE: Grandpa, look—look at me for a second. Try to remember my face.

DODGE: She wants to go. She just got here and she wants to go. Itchy.

VINCE: This is kind of strange for her. I mean, it's strange enough for me—

DODGE: She'll get used to it. (*To* SHELLY.) What part of the country do you hail from, girlie?

SHELLY: Originally?

DODGE: That's right. Originally. At the very start.

SHELLY: LA.

DODGE: LA. Stupid country.

SHELLY: I can't stand this, Vince! This is really unbelievable!

DODGE: It's stupid! LA is stupid! So is Florida. All those Sunshine States. They're all stupid! Do you know why they're stupid?

SHELLY: Illuminate me.

VINCE: Shelly. Don't!

DODGE: I'll tell you why. Because they're full of smart-asses! That's why. (SHELLY *turns her back to* DODGE, *crosses to staircase and sits on bottom step. To* VINCE.) Now she's insulted.

SHELLY: Vince?

DODGE: She's insulted! Look at her! In my house she's insulted! She's over there sulking because I insulted her!

VINCE: Grandpa—

SHELLY: (*To* VINCE.) This is really terrific. This is wonderful. And you were worried about me making the right first impression!

DODGE: (*To* VINCE.) She's a fireball, isn't she? Regular fireball. I had some a them in my day. Temporary stuff. Never lasted more than a week.

VINCE: Grandpa—look—

DODGE: Stop calling me Grandpa, will ya! It's sickening. "Grandpa." I'm nobody's grandpa! Least of all yours.

VINCE: I can't believe you don't recognize me. I just can't believe it. It wasn't that long ago. (DODGE *starts feeling around under the cushion for the bottle of whiskey.* SHELLY *gets up from the staircase.*)

SHELLY: (*To* VINCE.) Maybe you've got the wrong house. Did you ever think of that? Maybe this is the wrong address!

VINCE: It's not the wrong address! I recognize the yard. The porch. The elm tree. The house. I was standing right here in this house. Right in this very spot.

SHELLY: Yeah, but do you recognize the people? He says he's not your grandfather.

VINCE: He *is* my grandpa! I know he's my grandpa! He's *always* been my grandpa. He always *will be* my grandpa!

DODGE: (*Digging for the bottle.*) Where's that bottle?!

VINCE: He's just sick or something. I don't know what's happened to him. Delirious.

DODGE: Where's my goddamn bottle?! (DODGE *gets up from the sofa and starts tearing the cushions off it and throwing them downstage, looking for the whiskey.*) They've stole my bottle!

SHELLY: Can't we just drive on to New Mexico? This is terrible, Vince! I don't want to stay here. In this house. I thought it was going to be turkey dinners and apple pie and all that kinda stuff.

VINCE: Well, I hate to disappoint you!

SHELLY: I'm not disappointed! I'm fuckin' terrified! I wanna go! (DODGE *yells toward left.*)

DODGE: Tilden! Tilden! They stole my bottle! (DODGE *keeps ripping away at the sofa looking for his bottle. He knocks over the night stand with the bottles.* VINCE *and* SHELLY *watch as he starts ripping the stuffing out of the sofa.*)

VINCE: (*To* SHELLY.) He's lost his mind or something. I've got to try to help him.

SHELLY: You help him! I'm leaving! (SHELLY *starts to leave.* VINCE *grabs her. They struggle as* DODGE *keeps ripping away at the sofa and yelling.*)

DODGE: Tilden! Tilden, get your ass in here! Tilden!

SHELLY: Let go of me!

VINCE: You're not going anywhere! I need you to stay right here!

SHELLY: Let go of me, you sonuvabitch! I'm not your property! (*Suddenly* TILDEN *walks on from left just as he did before. This time his arms are full of carrots.* DODGE, VINCE, *and* SHELLY *stop suddenly when they see him. They all stare at* TILDEN *as he crosses slowly center with the carrots and stops.* DODGE *sits on the sofa, exhausted.*)

DODGE: (*Panting, to* TILDEN.) Where in the hell have you been?

TILDEN: Out back.

DODGE: Where's my bottle?

TILDEN: Gone. (TILDEN *and* VINCE *stare at each other.* SHELLY *backs away.*)

DODGE: (*To* TILDEN.) *You* stole my bottle!

VINCE: (*To* TILDEN.) Dad? What're you doing here?

SHELLY: Oh brother. (TILDEN *just stares at* VINCE.)

DODGE: You had no right to steal my bottle! No right at all! Who do you think you are?

VINCE: (*To* TILDEN.) It's Vince. I'm Vince. (TILDEN *stares at* VINCE, *then looks at* DODGE, *then turns to* SHELLY.)

TILDEN: (*After pause.*) I picked these carrots. If anybody wants any carrots, I picked 'em.

SHELLY: (*To* VINCE.) Now, wait a minute. This is your father? The one we were going to visit?

VINCE: (*To* TILDEN.) Dad, what're you doing here? What's going on? (TILDEN *just stares at* VINCE, *holding the carrots.* DODGE *pulls the blanket back over himself.*)

SHELLY: This is actually your father? The one in New Mexico?

DODGE: (*To* TILDEN.) You're going to have to get me another bottle! You gotta get me a bottle before Halie comes back! There's money on the table. (*Points to left kitchen.*)

TILDEN: (*Shaking his head.*) I'm not going down there. Into town. I never do well in town. (SHELLY *crosses to* TILDEN. TILDEN *stares at her.*)

SHELLY: (*To* TILDEN.) Are you Vince's father?

TILDEN: (*To* SHELLY.) Vince?

SHELLY: (*Pointing to* VINCE.) This is supposed to be your son! Is he your son? Do you recognize him? I'm just along for the ride here. I thought everybody knew each other! (TILDEN *stares at* VINCE. DODGE *wraps himself up in the blanket and sits on the sofa staring at the floor.*)

TILDEN: I had a son once but we buried him. (DODGE *quickly looks at* TILDEN. SHELLY *looks to* VINCE.)

DODGE: You shut up about that! You don't know anything about that!

VINCE: Dad, I thought you were in Bernalillo. We were going to drive down there and see you.

TILDEN: Long way to drive. Terrible distance.

VINCE: What's happened, Dad? Has something happened? I thought everything was all right. What's happened to Halie? What're you doing back here?

TILDEN: She left. Church or something. It's always church. God or Jesus. Or both.

SHELLY: (*To* TILDEN.) Do you want me to take those carrots for you?

VINCE: Shelly— (TILDEN *stares at her. She moves in close to him. Holds out her arms.* TILDEN *stares at her arms, then slowly dumps the carrots into her arms.* SHELLY *stands there holding the carrots.*)

TILDEN: (*To* SHELLY.) You like carrots?

SHELLY: Sure. I like all kinds of vegetables. I'm a vegetarian.

DODGE: (*To* TILDEN.) Hitler was a vegetarian. You gotta get me a bottle before Halie comes back! (DODGE *hits the sofa with his fist.* VINCE *crosses up to* DODGE *and tries to console him.* SHELLY *and* TILDEN *stay facing each other.*)

TILDEN: (*To* SHELLY.) Backyard's full of carrots. Corn. Potatoes.

SHELLY: You're Vince's father, right? His real father. I'm just asking.

TILDEN: All kinds of vegetables. You like vegetables?

SHELLY: (*Laughs.*) Yeah. I love vegetables.

TILDEN: We could cook these carrots, ya know. You could cut 'em up and we could cook 'em. You and me.

SHELLY: All right. Sure. Whatever works.

VINCE: Shelly, what're you doing?

TILDEN: I'll get you a pail and a knife.

SHELLY: Okay.

VINCE: Shelly!

TILDEN: I'll be right back. Don't go.

VINCE: Dad, wait a second. (TILDEN *exits off left.*) What the hell is going on here? What's happened to everybody? (SHELLY *stands center, arms full of carrots.* VINCE *stands next to* DODGE. SHELLY *looks toward* VINCE *then down at the carrots.*)

DODGE: (*To* VINCE.) You could get me a bottle. (*Pointing off left.*) There's money on the table.

VINCE: Grandpa, why don't you lay down for a while?

DODGE: I don't wanna lay down for a while! Every time I lay down something happens! (*Whips off his cap, points at his head.*) Look what happens! That's what happens! (*Pulls his cap back on.*) You go lay down and see what happens to you! See how you like it! They'll steal your bottle! They'll cut your hair! They'll murder your children! That's what'll happen. They'll eat you alive.

VINCE: Just relax for a while. Maybe things will come back to you. (*Pause.*)

DODGE: You could get me a bottle, ya know. There's nothing stopping you from getting me a bottle.

SHELLY: Why don't you get him a bottle, Vince? Maybe it would help everybody identify each other.

DODGE: (*Pointing to* SHELLY.) There, see? She thinks you should get me a bottle. She's a smart cookie. Suddenly, she got smart. (VINCE *crosses to* SHELLY.)

VINCE: Shelly, what're you doing with those carrots?

SHELLY: I'm waiting for your father.

DODGE: She thinks you should get me a bottle!

VINCE: Shelly, put the carrots down, will ya! We gotta deal with the situation here! I'm gonna need your help. I don't know what's going on here but I need some help to try to figure this out.

SHELLY: I'm helping.

VINCE: You're only adding to the problem! You're making things worse! Put the carrots down! (VINCE *tries to knock the carrots out of her arms. She turns away from him, protecting the carrots.*)

SHELLY: Get away from me! Stop it! (VINCE *stands back from her. She turns to him still holding the carrots.*)

VINCE: (*To* SHELLY.) Why are you doing this? Are you trying to make fun of me? This is my family, you know!

SHELLY: You coulda fooled me! I'd just as soon not be here myself. I'd just as soon be a thousand miles from here. I'd rather be anywhere but here. You're the one who wants to stay. So I'll stay. I'll stay and I'll cut the carrots. And I'll cook the carrots. And I'll do whatever I have to do to survive. Just to make it through this thing.

VINCE: Put the carrots down, Shelly. The carrots aren't going to help. The carrots have nothing to do with the situation here. (TILDEN *enters from left with the pail, the milking stool, and a knife. He sets the stool and pail center for* SHELLY. SHELLY *looks at* VINCE, *then sits down on the stool, sets the carrots on the floor, and takes the knife from* TILDEN. *She looks at Vince again, then picks up a carrot, cuts the ends off, scrapes it, and drops it in the pail. She repeats this.* VINCE *glares at her. She smiles.*)

DODGE: She could get me a bottle. She's the type a girl that could get me a bottle. Easy. She'd go down there. Slink up to the counter. They'd probably give her two bottles for the price of one. She could do that. She has that air about her. (SHELLY *laughs. Keeps cutting carrots.* VINCE *crosses up to* DODGE, *looks at him.* TILDEN *watches* SHELLY's *hands. Long pause.*)

VINCE: (*To* DODGE.) I haven't changed that much. I mean physically. Physically I'm just about the same. Same size. Same weight. Everything's the same. (DODGE *keeps staring at* SHELLY *while* VINCE *talks to him.*)

DODGE: She's a beautiful girl. Exceptional. (VINCE *moves in front of* DODGE *to block his view of* SHELLY. DODGE *keeps cran-*

ing his head around to see her as VINCE *demonstrates tricks from his past.*)

VINCE: Look. Look at this. Do you remember this? I used to bend my thumb behind my knuckles. You remember? I used to do it at the dinner table. Way back when. You told me, one day it would get stuck like this and I'd never be able to throw a baseball. (VINCE *bends a thumb behind his knuckles for* DODGE *and holds it out to him.* DODGE *takes a short glance, then looks back at* SHELLY. VINCE *shifts position and shows him something else.*) What about this? (VINCE *curls his lips back and starts drumming on his teeth with his fingernails, making little tapping sounds.* DODGE *watches a while.* TILDEN *turns toward the sound.* VINCE *keeps it up. He sees* TILDEN *taking notice and crosses to* TILDEN *as he drums on his teeth.* DODGE *turns the TV on and watches it.*) You remember this, Dad? Rooty-tooty? "St. James Infirmary"? "When the Saints Go Marching In"? (VINCE *keeps on drumming for* TILDEN. TILDEN *watches a while, fascinated, then turns back to* SHELLY. VINCE *keeps up the drumming on his teeth, crosses back to* DODGE *doing it.* SHELLY *keeps working on the carrots, talking to* TILDEN.)

SHELLY: (*To* TILDEN.) He drives me crazy with that some-times.

VINCE: (*To* DODGE.) I know! Here's one you'll remember. You used to kick me out of the house for this one. (VINCE *pulls his shirt out of his belt and holds it tucked under his chin with his stomach exposed. He grabs the flesh on either side of his belly button and pushes it in and out to make it look like a mouth talking. He watches his belly button and makes a deep-sounding cartoon voice to synchronize with the movement. He demonstrates it to* DODGE, *then crosses down to* TILDEN *doing it. Both* DODGE *and* TILDEN *take short, uninterested glances, then ignore him. Deep cartoon voice.)* "Hello. How are you? I'm fine. Thank you very much. It's so good to see you looking well this fine Sunday morning." It's the same old me. Same old dependable me. Never change. Never alter one iota. (VINCE *stops. Tucks his shirt back in.)*

SHELLY: Vince, don't be pathetic, will ya! They're not gonna play. Can't you see that? (SHELLY *keeps cutting carrots.* VINCE *slowly moves toward* TILDEN. TILDEN *keeps watching* SHELLY.)

VINCE: *(To* SHELLY.) I don't get it. I really don't get it. Maybe it's me. Maybe I forgot something.

DODGE: *(From the sofa.)* You forgot to get me a bottle! That's what you forgot. Anybody in this house could get me a bottle. Anybody! But nobody will. Nobody understands the urgency! Peelin' carrots is more important. Playin' piano on your teeth! Well, I hope you all remember this when you get up in years. When you find yourself immobilized. Dependent on the whims of others. (VINCE *moves up toward* DODGE. *Pause as* VINCE *looks at him.* SHELLY *continues cutting carrots. Pause.* VINCE *moves around, stroking his hair, staring at* DODGE *and* TILDEN. VINCE *and* SHELLY *exchange glances.* DODGE *watches TV.)*

VINCE: Boy! This is amazing. This is truly amazing. (*Keeps moving around.*) What is this anyway? Am I being punished here or what? Is that it? Some kind of banishment? Some kind of wicked warped exile? Just tell me. I can take it. Lay it on me. What was it? Did I betray some secret ancient family taboo, way back when? Did I cross the line somehow when I wasn't looking? What exactly was it?

SHELLY: Vince, what are you doing that for? They don't care about any of that. They just don't recognize you, that's all. They don't have a clue.

VINCE: How could they not recognize me?! How in the hell could they not recognize me?! I'm their son! I'm their flesh and blood. Anybody can see we're related.

DODGE: (*Watching TV.*) You're no son of mine. I've had sons in my time—plenty of sons—but you're not one of 'em. I know them by their scent. (*Long pause.* VINCE *stares at* DODGE.)

VINCE: All right. All right, look—I'll get you a bottle. I'll get you a goddamn bottle.

DODGE: You will?

VINCE: Yeah, sure, you bet. If that's what it takes, I'll get you a bottle. Then maybe you can tell me what's going on here.

SHELLY: You're not going to leave me here alone, are you?

VINCE: (*Moving to her.*) You suggested it! You said, "Why don't I go get him a bottle." So I'll go get him a bottle! That's what I'll do. Maybe it'll help jar things loose.

SHELLY: But I can't stay here by myself.

DODGE: Don't let her talk you out of it! She's a bad influence. I could see it the minute she stepped in here.

VINCE: Shelly, I gotta go out for a while. I just gotta get outta here. Think things through by myself. I'll get a bottle and I'll come right back.

SHELLY: I don't know if I can handle this, Vince.

VINCE: You'll be okay. Nothing's going to happen. They're not dangerous or anything.

SHELLY: Can't we just go?

VINCE: No! I gotta find out what's going on here. Something has fallen apart. This isn't how it used to be. Believe me. This is nothing like how it used to be . . .

SHELLY: Look, you think you're bad off, what about me? Not only don't they recognize me but I've never seen them before in my life. I don't know who these guys are. They could be anybody!

VINCE: They're not anybody!

SHELLY: That's what you say.

VINCE: They're my family for Christ's sake! I should know who my own family is! Now give me a break. It won't take that long. I'll just go out and I'll come right back. Nothing'll happen. I promise. (SHELLY *stares at him. Pause.*)

SHELLY: Unbelievable.

VINCE: Nothing'll happen. (*He crosses up to* DODGE.) I'm gonna go out now, Grandpa, and I'll pick you up a bottle. Okay?

DODGE: Persistence, see? That's what it takes. Persistence. Persistence, fortitude, and determination. Those are the three virtues. That's how the country was *founded*. You stick with those three and you can't go wrong. (*Pointing off left.*) Money's on the table. In the kitchen. (VINCE *moves toward* SHELLY.)

VINCE: (*To* SHELLY.) You'll be all right, Shelly. I won't be too long.

SHELLY: (*Cutting carrots.*) I'll just keep real busy while you're gone. I love vegetables. (VINCE *exits.* TILDEN *keeps staring down at* SHELLY*'s hands.*)

VINCE: (*Reentering, to* TILDEN.) You want anything, Dad?

TILDEN: (*Looks up at* VINCE.) Me?

VINCE: Yeah, you. "Dad." That's you. From the store? I'm gonna get Grandpa a bottle. Do you want anything from the store?

TILDEN: He's not supposed to drink. Halie wouldn't like it. She'd be disappointed.

VINCE: He wants a bottle.

TILDEN: He's not supposed to drink.

DODGE: (*To* VINCE.) Don't negotiate with him! He's the one who stole my bottle! Don't make any transactions until you've spoken to me first! He'll steal you blind!

VINCE: (*To* DODGE.) Tilden says you're not supposed to drink.

DODGE: Tilden's lost his marbles! Look at him! He's around the twist. Take a look at him. He's come unwound. (VINCE *stares at* TILDEN. TILDEN *watches* SHELLY's *hands as she keeps cutting carrots.*) Now look at me. Look here at me! (VINCE *looks back to* DODGE.) Now, between the two of us, who do you think is more trustworthy? Him or me? Can you trust a man who keeps bringing in vegetables from out of nowhere? Take a look at him. (VINCE *looks back at* TILDEN.)

SHELLY: Go get the bottle, Vince. Just go get the bottle.

VINCE: I'll be right back. (VINCE *crosses left.*)

DODGE: Where are you going?

VINCE: I'm going to get the money.

DODGE: Then where are you goin'?

VINCE: Liquor store.

DODGE: Don't go off anyplace else. Don't go off someplace and drink by yourself. Come right back here.

VINCE: I will. (VINCE *exits left.*)

DODGE: (*Calling after* VINCE.) You've got responsibility now! And don't go out the back way either! Come out through this way! I wanna see you when you leave! Don't go out the back.

VINCE: (*Off left.*) I won't! (DODGE *turns and looks at* TILDEN *and* SHELLY.)

DODGE: Untrustworthy. Probably drown himself if he went out the back. Fall right in a hole. I'd never get my bottle.

SHELLY: I wouldn't worry about Vince. He can take care of himself.

DODGE: Oh he can, huh? Independent. (VINCE *comes on again from left with two dollars in his hand. He crosses right past* DODGE. *To* VINCE.) You got the money?

VINCE: Yeah. Two bucks.

DODGE: Two bucks. Two bucks is two bucks. Don't sneer.

VINCE: What kind do you want for two bucks?

DODGE: Whiskey! Gold Star Sour Mash. Use your own discretion.

VINCE: Okay.

DODGE: Nothin' fancy! (VINCE *crosses to right door. Opens it. Stops when he hears* TILDEN.)

TILDEN: (*To* VINCE.) You drove all the way from New Mexico?

VINCE: (*From the porch.*) No, I—look—while I'm gone, try to remember who I am. Try real hard to remember. Use your imagination. It might suddenly come back to you. In a flash. (VINCE *turns and looks at* TILDEN. *They stare at each other.* VINCE *shakes his head, goes out the door, crosses the porch, and exits out the screen door.* TILDEN *watches him go. Pause.*)

TILDEN: That's a long, lonely stretch of road. I've driven that stretch before and there's no end to it. You feel like you're going to fall right off into blackness.

SHELLY: You really don't recognize him? Either one of you? (TILDEN *turns again and stares at* SHELLY's *hands as she cuts carrots.*)

DODGE: (*Watching TV.*) Recognize who?

SHELLY: Vince.

DODGE: What's to recognize? (DODGE *lights a cigarette, coughs slightly, and stares at the TV.*)

SHELLY: It'd be cruel if you recognized him and didn't tell him. Wouldn't be fair.

DODGE: Cruel.

SHELLY: Well, it would be. I mean it's not really possible, is it, that he's not related to you at all? Just a stranger? He seems so sure about it. (DODGE *just stares at the TV, smoking.*)

TILDEN: I thought I recognized him. I thought I recognized something about him.

SHELLY: You did?

TILDEN: I thought I saw a face inside his face.

SHELLY: Well, it was probably that you saw what he used to look like. You haven't seen him for six years.

TILDEN: I haven't?

SHELLY: That's what he says. (TILDEN *moves around in front of her as she continues with the carrots.*)

TILDEN: Where was it I saw him last?

SHELLY: I have no idea. I've only known him for a few months, myself. He doesn't tell me everything.

TILDEN: He doesn't?

SHELLY: Not stuff like that.

TILDEN: What does he tell you?

SHELLY: You mean in general?

TILDEN: Yeah. (TILDEN *moves around behind her.*)

SHELLY: Well, he tells me all kinds of things.

TILDEN: Like what?

SHELLY: I don't know! I mean I can't just come out and tell you how he feels.

TILDEN: How come? (TILDEN *keeps moving around her slowly in a circle.*)

SHELLY: Because it's stuff he told me privately!

TILDEN: And you can't tell me?

SHELLY: I don't even know you! I'm not even sure *he* knows you.

DODGE: Tilden, go out in the kitchen and make me some coffee! Leave the girl alone. She's nervous. She's ready to jump ship any second.

SHELLY: (*To* DODGE.) He's all right. (TILDEN *ignores* DODGE, *keeps moving around* SHELLY. *He stares at her hair and coat.* DODGE *stares at the TV.*)

TILDEN: You mean you can't tell me anything?

SHELLY: I can tell you some things. I mean we can have a conversation.

TILDEN: We can?

SHELLY: Sure. We're having a conversation right now.

TILDEN: We are?

SHELLY: Yes. That's what we're doing. It's easy.

TILDEN: But there's certain things you can't tell me, right?

SHELLY: Right.

TILDEN: There's certain things I can't tell you either.

SHELLY: How come?

TILDEN: I don't know. Nobody's supposed to hear it.

SHELLY: Well, you can tell me anything you want to.

TILDEN: I can?

SHELLY: Sure.

TILDEN: It might not be very nice.

SHELLY: That's all right. I've been around.

TILDEN: It might be awful.

SHELLY: Well, can't you tell me anything nice? (TILDEN *stops in front of her and stares at her coat.* SHELLY *looks back at him. Long pause.*)

TILDEN: (*After pause.*) Can I touch your coat?

SHELLY: My coat? (*She looks at her coat then back to* TILDEN.) Sure.

TILDEN: You don't mind?

SHELLY: No. Go ahead. (SHELLY *holds her arm out for* TILDEN *to touch.* DODGE *stays fixed on the TV.* TILDEN *moves in slowly toward* SHELLY, *staring at her arm. He reaches out very slowly and touches her arm, feels the fur gently, then draws his hand back.* SHELLY *keeps her arm out.*) It's rabbit.

TILDEN: Rabbit. (*He reaches out again very slowly and touches the fur on her arm, then pulls back his hand again.* SHELLY *drops her arm.*)

SHELLY: My arm was getting tired.

TILDEN: Can I hold it? (*Pause.*)

SHELLY: The coat? Sure. I guess. (SHELLY *takes off her coat and hands it to* TILDEN. TILDEN *takes it slowly, feels the fur, then puts it on.* SHELLY *watches as* TILDEN *strokes the fur slowly. He smiles at her. She goes back to cutting carrots.*) You can have it if you want.

TILDEN: I can?

SHELLY: Yeah. I've got a raincoat in the car. That's all I need.

TILDEN: You've got a car?

SHELLY: Vince does. (TILDEN *walks around stroking the fur and smiling at the coat.* SHELLY *watches him when he's not looking.* DODGE *sticks with the TV, stretches out on the sofa wrapped in the blanket.*)

TILDEN: (*As he walks around.*) I had a car once! I had a white car! I drove. I went everywhere. I went to the mountains. I drove in the snow.

SHELLY: That must've been fun.

TILDEN: (*Still moving, feeling the coat.*) I drove all day long sometimes. Across the desert. Way out across the desert. I drove past tiny towns. Anywhere. Past palm trees. Lightning. Anything. I would drive through it. I would drive through it and I would stop and I would look around and I would see things sometimes. I would see things I wasn't supposed to see. Like deer. Hawks. Owls. I would look them in the eye and they would look back and I could tell I wasn't supposed to be there by the way they looked at me. So I'd drive on. I would get back in and drive! I loved to drive. There was nothing I loved more. Nothing I dreamed of was better than driving. I was independent.

DODGE: (*Eyes on the TV.*) Pipe down, would ya! Stop running off at the mouth. (TILDEN *stops. Stares at* SHELLY.)

SHELLY: Do you do much driving now?

TILDEN: Now? Now? I don't drive now.

SHELLY: How come?

TILDEN: I'm older.

SHELLY: You're not that old.

TILDEN: I'm not a kid.

SHELLY: You don't have to be a kid to drive.

TILDEN: It wasn't driving then.

SHELLY: What was it?

TILDEN: Adventure. I went everywhere. I had a sensation of myself.

SHELLY: Well, you can still do that.

TILDEN: Not now.

SHELLY: Why not?

TILDEN: I just told you. You don't understand. If I told you something you wouldn't understand it.

SHELLY: Told me what?

TILDEN: Told you something that's true.

SHELLY: Like what?

TILDEN: Like a baby. Like a little tiny baby.

SHELLY: Like when you were little?

TILDEN: If I told you you'd make me give your coat back.

SHELLY: I won't. I promise. Tell me. Please.

TILDEN: I can't. Dodge won't let me.

SHELLY: He won't hear you. It's okay. He's watching TV. (*Pause.* TILDEN *stares at her. Moves slightly toward her.*)

TILDEN: We had a baby. Little baby. Could pick it up with one hand. Put it in the other. (TILDEN *moves closer to her.* DODGE *takes more interest.*) So small that nobody could find it. Just disappeared. We had no service. No hymn. Nobody came.

DODGE: Tilden!

TILDEN: Cops looked for it. Neighbors. Nobody could find it. (DODGE *struggles to get up from the sofa.*)

DODGE: Tilden? You leave that girl alone! She's completely innocent. (DODGE *keeps struggling until he's standing.*)

TILDEN: Finally everybody just gave up. Just stopped looking. Everybody had a different answer. (DODGE *struggles to walk toward* TILDEN *and falls.* TILDEN *ignores him.*)

DODGE: Tilden! What are you telling her? (DODGE *starts coughing on the floor.* SHELLY *watches him from the stool.*)

TILDEN: Little tiny baby just disappeared. It's not hard. It's so small. Almost invisible. Hold it in one hand. (SHELLY *makes a move to help* DODGE. TILDEN *firmly pushes her back down on the stool.* DODGE *keeps coughing.*)

DODGE: Tilden! Don't tell her anything! She's an outsider!

TILDEN: He's the only one who knows where it is. The only one. Like a secret buried treasure. Won't tell any of us. (DODGE*'s coughing subsides.* SHELLY *stays on the stool staring at* DODGE. TILDEN *slowly takes* SHELLY*'s coat off and holds it out to her. Long pause.* SHELLY *sits there trembling.*) You probably want your coat back now. I would if I was you. (SHELLY *stares at the coat but doesn't move to take it. The sound of* BRADLEY*'s leg squeaking is heard off left. The others onstage remain still.* BRADLEY *appears up left outside the screen door wearing a yellow rain slicker. He enters through the screen door, crosses the porch to the right door, and enters the stage. Closes the door.*

Takes off the rain slicker and shakes it out. He sees all the others and stops. TILDEN *turns to him.* BRADLEY *stares at* SHELLY. DODGE *remains on the floor.*)

BRADLEY: What's going on here? (*Motioning to* SHELLY.) Who's that? (SHELLY *stands, moves back away from* BRADLEY *as he crosses toward her. He stops next to* TILDEN. *He sees the coat in* TILDEN's *hand and grabs it away from him.*) Who's she supposed to be?

TILDEN: She's driving to New Mexico. She has a car. (BRADLEY *stares at her.* SHELLY *is frozen.* BRADLEY *limps over to her with the coat in his fist. He stops in front of her.*)

BRADLEY: (*To* SHELLY, *after pause.*) Vacation? (SHELLY *shakes her head "no," trembling. To* SHELLY, *motioning to* TILDEN.) You taking him with you? (SHELLY *shakes her head "no."* BRADLEY *crosses back to* TILDEN.) You oughta. No use leaving him here. Doesn't do a lick a work. Doesn't raise a finger. (*Stopping, to* TILDEN.) Do ya? (*To* SHELLY.) 'Course he used to be a All-American. Quarterback or fullback or somethin'.

TILDEN: Halfback.

BRADLEY: He tell you about that? Brag on himself? (SHELLY *shakes her head "no."*) Yeah, he used to be a big deal. Wore letterman's sweaters. Had medals hanging all around his neck. Real purty. Big damn deal. (*He laughs to himself, notices* DODGE *on the floor, crosses to him, stops.*) This one too. (*To* SHELLY.) You'd never think it to look at him, would ya? All paunchy and bloated. (SHELLY *shakes her head again.* BRADLEY *stares at her, crosses back to her, clenching the coat in his fist. He stops in front of* SHELLY.) Women like that kinda thing, don't they?

SHELLY: What?

BRADLEY: Importance. Importance in a man.

SHELLY: I don't know.

BRADLEY: Yeah. Ya know, ya know. Don't give me that. (*Moves closer to* SHELLY.) You're with Tilden?

SHELLY: No.

BRADLEY: (*Turning to* TILDEN.) Tilden! She with you? (TILDEN *doesn't answer. Stares at the floor.*) Tilden! You're gonna run now. Run like a scalded dog! (TILDEN *suddenly bolts and runs off up left.* BRADLEY *laughs. Talks to* SHELLY. DODGE *starts moving his lips silently as though talking to someone invisible on the floor. Laughing.*) Scared to death! He was always scared. Scared of his own shadow. (BRADLEY *stops laughing. Stares at* SHELLY.) Some things are like that. They just tremble for no reason. Ever noticed that? They just shake? (SHELLY *looks at* DODGE *on the floor.*)

SHELLY: Can't we do something for him?

BRADLEY: (*Looking at* DODGE.) We could shoot him. (*Laughs.*) Put him out of his misery.

SHELLY: Shut up! (BRADLEY *stops laughing. Moves in closer to* SHELLY. *She freezes.* BRADLEY *speaks slowly and deliberately.*)

BRADLEY: Hey! Missus. Don't talk to me like that. Don't talk to me in that tone a voice. There was a time when I had to take that tone a voice from pretty near everyone. (*Motioning to* DODGE.) Him, for one! When he was a whole man. Full of himself. Him and that half-brain that just ran outta here. They don't talk to me like that now. Not anymore. Everything's turned around now. Full circle. Isn't that funny?

SHELLY: I'm sorry.

BRADLEY: Open your mouth.

SHELLY: What?

BRADLEY: (*Motioning for her to open her mouth.*) Open up. (*She opens her mouth slightly.*) Wider. (*She opens her mouth wider.*) Keep it like that. (*She does. Stares at* BRADLEY. *With his free hand he puts his fingers into her mouth. She tries to pull away.*) Just stay put! (*She freezes. He keeps his fingers in her mouth. Stares at her. Pause. He pulls his hand out. She closes her mouth, keeps her eyes on him.* BRADLEY *smiles. He looks at* DODGE *on the floor and crosses over to him.* SHELLY *watches him closely.* BRADLEY *stands over* DODGE *and smiles at* SHELLY. *He holds her coat up in both hands over* DODGE, *keeps smiling at* SHELLY. *He looks down at* DODGE, *then drops the coat so that it lands on* DODGE *and covers his head.* BRADLEY *keeps his hands up in the position of holding the coat, looks over at* SHELLY, *and smiles. The lights black out.*)

Act Three

Scene: same set. Morning. Bright sun. No sound of rain. Everything has been cleared up again. No sign of carrots. No pail. No stool. VINCE's saxophone case and overcoat are still at the foot of the staircase. BRADLEY is asleep on the sofa under DODGE's blanket, his head toward stage left. BRADLEY's wooden leg is leaning against the sofa right by his head. The shoe is left on. The harness hangs down. DODGE is sitting on the floor, propped up against the TV set facing stage left, wearing his baseball cap. SHELLY's rabbit fur coat covers his chest and shoulders. He stares toward stage left. He seems weaker and more disoriented. The lights rise slowly to the sound of birds. The two men remain for a while in silence. BRADLEY sleeps very soundly. DODGE hardly moves. SHELLY appears from stage left with a big smile, slowly crossing toward DODGE balancing a steaming cup of broth in a saucer. DODGE just stares at her as she gets close to him.

SHELLY: (*As she crosses.*) This is going to make all the difference in the world, Grandpa. You don't mind me calling you Grandpa, do you? I mean I know you minded when Vince called you that but you don't even know him.

83

DODGE: I'm nobody's Grandpa. He skipped town with my money, you know. I'm gonna hold you as collateral.

SHELLY: He'll be back. Don't you worry. He always comes back.

DODGE: The faithful type.

SHELLY: No. Determined. (*She kneels down next to* DODGE *and puts the cup and saucer in his lap.*)

DODGE: It's morning already! When did it get to be morning? Not only didn't I get my bottle but he's got my two bucks! I'm surrounded by thieves.

SHELLY: Try to drink this, okay? Don't spill it.

DODGE: What is it?

SHELLY: Beef bouillon. It'll warm you up.

DODGE: Bouillon! I don't want any goddamn bouillon! Get that stuff away from me!

SHELLY: I just got through making it.

DODGE: I don't care if you just spent all week making it! I ain't drinking it!

SHELLY: Well, what am I supposed to do with it? I'm trying to help you out. Besides, it's good for you.

DODGE: Get it away from me! (SHELLY *stands up with the cup and saucer.*) What do you know what's good for me anyway? (*She looks at* DODGE, *then turns away from him, crosses to the staircase, sits on the bottom step, and drinks the bouillon.* DODGE *stares at her.*) You know what'd be good for me?

SHELLY: What?

DODGE: A little back rub. A little contact.

SHELLY: Oh no. I've had enough contact for a while. Thanks anyway. (*She keeps sipping the bouillon, stays sitting. Pause as* DODGE *stares at her.*)

DODGE: Why not? You got nothing better to do. That fella's not gonna be back here. You're not expecting him to show up again, are you?

SHELLY: Sure. He'll show up. He left his horn here.

DODGE: His horn? (*Laughs.*) You're his horn?

SHELLY: Very funny.

DODGE: He's run off with my money! That's what he did. He's not coming back here.

SHELLY: He'll be back. This is where he's from. He knows that. He's convinced. And so am I.

DODGE: You're a funny chicken, you know that?

SHELLY: Funny?

DODGE: Full of hope. Faith. Faith and hope. You're all alike, you hopers. If it's not God then it's a man. If it's not a man then it's a woman. If it's not a woman then it's politics or bee pollen or the future of some kind. Some kind of future.

SHELLY: Bee pollen?

DODGE: Yeah, bee pollen. (*Pause.*)

SHELLY: (*Looking toward the porch.*) I'm glad it stopped raining. (DODGE *looks toward the porch then back to* SHELLY.)

DODGE: That's what I mean. See, you're glad it stopped raining. Now you think everything's gonna be different. Just 'cause the sun comes out.

SHELLY: It's already different. Last night I was scared.

DODGE: Scared a what?

SHELLY: Just scared.

DODGE: Yeah, well we've all got an instinct for disaster. We can smell it coming.

SHELLY: It was your son. Bradley. He scared me.

DODGE: Bradley? (*Looks at* BRADLEY.) He's a pushover. 'Specially now. All ya gotta do is take his leg and throw it out the back door. Helpless. Totally helpless. (SHELLY *turns and stares at* BRADLEY's *wooden leg, then looks at* DODGE. *She sips bouillon.*)

SHELLY: You'd do that?

DODGE: Me? I've hardly got the strength to breathe.

SHELLY: But you'd actually do it if you could?

DODGE: Don't be so easily shocked, girlie. There's nothing a man can't do. You dream it up and he can do it. Anything. It boggles the imagination.

SHELLY: You've tried, I guess.

DODGE: Don't sit there sippin' your bouillon and judging me! This is my house!

SHELLY: I forgot.

DODGE: You forgot? Whose house did you think it was?

SHELLY: Mine. (DODGE *just stares at her. Long pause. She sips from the cup.*) I know it's not mine but I had that feeling.

DODGE: What feeling?

SHELLY: The feeling that nobody lives here but me. I mean everybody's gone. You're here, but it doesn't seem like you're supposed to be. (*Pointing to* BRADLEY.) Doesn't seem like he's supposed to be here either. I don't know what it is. It's the house or something. Something familiar. Like I know my way around here. Did you ever get that feeling? (DODGE *stares at her in silence. Pause.*)

DODGE: No. No, I never did. I get lost in the hallway some-times. (SHELLY *gets up. Moves around the space holding the cup.*)

SHELLY: Last night I went to sleep up there in that room.

DODGE: What room?

SHELLY: That room up there with all the pictures. All the crosses on the wall.

DODGE: Halie's room?

SHELLY: Yeah. Whoever "Halie" is.

DODGE: She's my wife.

SHELLY: So you remember her?

DODGE: Whadya mean? 'Course I remember her. She's only been gone a day—half a day. However long it's been.

SHELLY: Do you remember her when her hair was bright red? Standing in front of an apple tree?

DODGE: What is this, the third degree or something?! Who're you to be askin' me personal questions about my wife!

SHELLY: You never look at those pictures up there?

DODGE: What pictures?

SHELLY: Your whole life's up there hanging on the wall. Somebody who looks just like you. Somebody who looks just like you used to look.

DODGE: That isn't me! That never was me! This is me. Right here. This is it. The whole shootin' match, sittin' right here in front of you. That other stuff was a sham.

SHELLY: So the past never happened as far as you're concerned?

DODGE: The past? Jesus Christ. The past is passed. What do you know about the past?

SHELLY: Not much. I know there was a farm. (*Pause.*)

DODGE: A farm?

SHELLY: There's a picture of a farm. A big farm. A bull. Wheat. Corn.

DODGE: Corn?

SHELLY: All the kids are standing out in the corn. They're all waving these big straw hats. One of them doesn't have a hat.

DODGE: Which one was that?

SHELLY: There's a baby. A baby in a woman's arms. The same woman with the red hair. She looks lost standing out there. Like she doesn't know how she got there.

DODGE: She knows! I told her a hundred times it wasn't gonna be the city! I gave her plenty a warning.

SHELLY: She's looking down at the baby like it was somebody else's. Like it didn't even belong to her.

DODGE: That's about enough outta you! You got some funny ideas, sister. Some damn funny ideas. You think just because people propagate they have to love their offspring? You never seen a bitch eat her puppies? Where are you from anyway?

SHELLY: LA. We already went through that.

DODGE: That's right, LA. I remember.

SHELLY: Stupid country.

DODGE: That's right! No wonder. Dumber than dirt. (*Pause.*)

SHELLY: What's happened to this family anyway?

DODGE: You're in no position to ask! What do you care? You some kinda social worker?

SHELLY: I'm Vince's friend.

DODGE: Vince's friend! That's rich. That's real rich. "Vince"! "Mr. Vince"! "Mr. Thief" is more like it! His name doesn't mean a hoot in hell to me. Not a tinkle in the well. You know how many kids I've spawned? Not to mention grandkids and great-grandkids and great-great-grandkids after them?

SHELLY: And you don't remember any of them?

DODGE: What's to remember? Halie's the one with the family album. She's the one you should talk to. She'll set you straight on the heritage if that's what you're interested in. She's traced it all the way back to the grave.

SHELLY: What do you mean?

DODGE: What do you think I mean? How far back can you go? A long line of corpses! There's not a living soul behind me. Not a one. Who gives a damn about bones in the ground?

SHELLY: What was Tilden trying to tell me last night? (DODGE *stops short. Stares at* SHELLY. *Shakes his head. He looks off left.* DODGE's *tone changes drastically.*)

DODGE: Tilden? (*Turns to* SHELLY, *calmly.*) Where is Tilden?

SHELLY: What was he trying to say about the baby? (*Pause.* DODGE *turns toward left.*)

DODGE: What's happened to Tilden? Why isn't Tilden here?

SHELLY: Bradley chased him out.

DODGE: (*Looking at* BRADLEY *asleep.*) Bradley? Why is he on my sofa? (*Turns back to* SHELLY.) Have I been here all night? On the floor?

SHELLY: He wouldn't leave. I hid outside until he fell asleep.

DODGE: Outside? Is Tilden outside? He shouldn't be out there in the rain. He'll get himself into trouble. He doesn't know his way around here anymore. Not like he used to. He went out West and got himself into trouble. Deep trouble. We don't want any of that around here.

SHELLY: What did he do? (*Pause.*)

DODGE: (*Quietly stares at* SHELLY.) Tilden? He got mixed up. That's what he did. We can't afford to leave him alone. Not now. (*Sound of* HALIE *laughing comes from off left.* SHELLY *stands, looking in the direction of the voice, holding the cup and saucer, doesn't know whether to stay or run. Motioning to* SHELLY.) Sit down! Sit back down! (SHELLY *sits. Sound of* HALIE'*s laughter again. To* SHELLY *in a heavy whisper, pulling the coat up around him.*) Don't leave me alone now! Promise me? Don't go off and leave me alone. I need somebody here with me. Tilden's gone now and I need someone. Don't leave me! Promise!

SHELLY: (*Sitting.*) I won't. (HALIE *appears outside the screen porch door, up left, with* FATHER DEWIS. *She is wearing a bright yellow*

dress, no hat, and white gloves, and her arms are full of yellow roses.
FATHER DEWIS *is dressed in a traditional black suit, white cleri-cal collar, and shirt. He is a very distinguished gray-haired man in his sixties. They are both slightly drunk and feeling giddy. As they enter the porch through the screen door,* DODGE *pulls the rabbit fur coat over his head and hides.* SHELLY *stands again.* DODGE *drops the coat and whispers intently to* SHELLY. *Neither* HALIE *nor* FATHER DEWIS *is aware of the people inside the house.)*

DODGE: *(To* SHELLY *in a strong whisper.)* You promised! *(*SHELLY *sits on the stairs again.* DODGE *pulls the coat back over his head.* HALIE *and* FATHER DEWIS *talk on the porch as they cross toward the right interior door.)*

HALIE: Oh, Father! That's terrible! That's absolutely terrible! Aren't you afraid of being punished? *(She giggles.)*

DEWIS: Not by the Italians. They're too busy punishing each other. *(They both break out in giggles.)*

HALIE: What about God?

DEWIS: Well, prayerfully, God only hears what he wants to. That's just between you and me of course. In our heart of hearts we know we're every bit as wicked as the Catholics. *(They giggle again and reach the right door.)*

HALIE: Father, I never heard you talk like this in Sunday sermon.

DEWIS: Well, I save all my best jokes for private company. Pearls before swine, you know. *(They enter the room laughing and stop when they see* SHELLY. SHELLY *stands.* HALIE *closes the door behind* FATHER DEWIS. DODGE'*s voice is heard under the coat talking to* SHELLY.)

DODGE: (*Under the coat, to* SHELLY.) Sit down, sit down! Don't let 'em buffalo you. (SHELLY *sits on the stair again.* HALIE *looks at* DODGE *on the floor, then looks at* BRADLEY *asleep on the sofa and sees his wooden leg. She lets out a shriek of embarrassment for* FATHER DEWIS.)

HALIE: Oh my gracious! What in the name of Judas Priest is going on in this house?! (*She hands over the roses to* FATHER DEWIS.) Excuse me, Father. (HALIE *crosses to* DODGE, *whips the coat off him, and covers the wooden leg with it.* BRADLEY *stays asleep.*) You can't leave this house for a second without the devil blowing in the front door!

DODGE: Gimme back that coat! Gimme back that goddamn coat before I freeze to death!

HALIE: You're not going to freeze! The sun's out in case you hadn't noticed!

DODGE: Gimme back that coat! That coat's for live flesh not dead wood. (HALIE *whips the blanket off* BRADLEY *and throws it on* DODGE. DODGE *covers his head again with the blanket.* BRADLEY'*s amputated leg can be faked by having it under a cushion on the sofa.* BRADLEY'*s fully clothed. He sits up with a jerk when the blanket comes off him.*)

HALIE: (*As she tosses the blanket.*) Here! Use this! It's yours anyway! Can't you take care of yourself for once?!

BRADLEY: (*Yelling at* HALIE.) Gimme that blanket! Gimme back that blanket! That's my blanket! (HALIE *crosses back toward* FATHER DEWIS, *who just stands there with the roses.* BRADLEY *thrashes helplessly on the sofa trying to reach the blanket.* DODGE *hides himself deeper in the blanket.* SHELLY *looks on from the staircase, still holding the cup and saucer.*)

HALIE: Believe me, Father, this is not what I had in mind when I invited you in. I keep forgetting how easily things fall to pieces when I'm not here to hold them together.

DEWIS: Oh, no apologies please. I wouldn't be in the ministry if I couldn't face real life. (FATHER DEWIS *laughs self-consciously.* HALIE *notices* SHELLY *again and crosses over to her.* SHELLY *stays sitting.* HALIE *stops and stares at her.*)

BRADLEY: I want my blanket back! Gimme my blanket! (HALIE *turns toward* BRADLEY *and silences him.*)

HALIE: Shut up, Bradley! Right this minute. I've had enough! It's shameful the way you carry on. (BRADLEY *slowly recoils, lies back down on the sofa, turns his back toward* HALIE, *and whimpers softly.* HALIE *directs her attention to* SHELLY *again. Pause.*)

BRADLEY: You gave me that blanket.

HALIE: Enough. (*To* SHELLY.) What are you doing with my cup and saucer?

SHELLY: (*Looking at the cup, back to* HALIE.) I made some bouillon for Dodge.

HALIE: For Dodge?

SHELLY: Yeah.

HALIE: My husband, Dodge.

SHELLY: Yes.

HALIE: You're here in my house making bouillon for my husband.

SHELLY: Yes.

HALIE: Well, did he drink it?

SHELLY: No.

HALIE: Did you drink it?

SHELLY: Yes. (HALIE *stares at her. Long pause. She turns abruptly away from* SHELLY *and crosses back to* FATHER DEWIS.)

HALIE: Father, there's a stranger in my house. What would you advise? What would be the Christian thing?

DEWIS: (*Squirming.*) Oh, well . . . I . . . I really—is she a trespasser?

HALIE: We still have some whiskey, don't we? A drop or two? (DODGE *slowly pulls the blanket down and looks toward* FATHER DEWIS. SHELLY *stands.*)

SHELLY: Listen, I don't drink or anything. I just— (HALIE *turns toward* SHELLY *viciously.*)

HALIE: You sit back down! (SHELLY *sits again on the stair.* HALIE *turns again to* DEWIS.) I think we still have plenty of whiskey left! Don't we, Father?

DEWIS: Well, yes. I think so. You'll have to get it. My hands are full. (HALIE *giggles. Reaches into* DEWIS*'s pockets, searching for the bottle. She smells the roses as she searches.* DEWIS *stands stiffly.* DODGE *watches* HALIE *closely as she looks for the bottle.*)

HALIE: Roses. The most incredible things, roses! Aren't they incredible, Father?

DEWIS: Yes. Yes they are.

HALIE: They almost cover the stench of sin in this house. Hanky-panky. Just magnificent! The smell. We'll have to put some at the foot of Ansel's statue. On the day of the unveiling. (HALIE *finds a silver flask of whiskey in* DEWIS*'s vest pocket. She pulls it out.* DODGE *looks on eagerly.* HALIE *crosses to* DODGE, *opens the flask, and takes a sip. To* DODGE.) Ansel's getting a statue, Dodge. Did you know that? Not a plaque but a real live statue. A full bronze. Tip to toe. A basketball in one hand and a rifle in the other.

BRADLEY: (*His back to* HALIE.) He never played basketball!

HALIE: You better shut up, Bradley! You shut up about Ansel! Ansel played basketball better than anyone! And you know it! He was an All-American! There's no reason to take the glory away from others. Especially when one's own shortcomings are so apparent. (HALIE *turns away from* BRADLEY, *crosses back toward* DEWIS, *sipping on the flask and smiling. To* DEWIS.) Ansel was a great basketball player. Make no mistake. One of the greatest.

DEWIS: I remember Ansel. Handsome lad. Tall and strapping.

HALIE: Of course! You remember. You remember how he could play. (*She turns toward* SHELLY.) Of course, nowadays they play a different brand of basketball. More vicious. Isn't that right, dear?

SHELLY: I don't know. (HALIE *crosses to* SHELLY, *sipping on the flask. She stops in front of* SHELLY.)

HALIE: Much, much more vicious. They smash into each other. They knock each other's teeth out. There's blood all over the court. Savages. Barbaric, don't you think? (HALIE *takes the cup from* SHELLY *and pours whiskey into it.*) They don't train like they used to. Not at all. They allow themselves to run amok. Drugs and women. Women mostly. (HALIE *hands the cup of whiskey back to* SHELLY *slowly.* SHELLY *takes it.*) Mostly women. Girls. Sad, pathetic little skinny girls. (*She crosses back to* FATHER DEWIS.) It's just a reflection of the times, don't you think, Father? An indication of where we stand?

DEWIS: I suppose so, yes. I've been so busy with the choir—

HALIE: Yes. A sort of bad omen. Our youth becoming monsters.

DEWIS: Well, I uh—wouldn't go quite that far.

HALIE: Oh, you can disagree with me if you want to, Father.
I'm open to debate. (*She moves toward* DODGE.) I suppose,
in the long run, it doesn't matter. When you see the
way things deteriorate before your very eyes. Everything
running downhill. It's kind of silly to even think about
youth.

DEWIS: No, I don't think so. I think it's important to believe
in certain things. Certain basic truths. I mean—

HALIE: Yes. Yes, I know what you mean. I think that's right. I
think that's true. (*She looks at* DODGE.) Certain basic
things. We can't shake the fundamentals. We might end up
crazy. Like my husband. You can see it in his eyes. You can
see the madness almost oozing out. (DODGE *covers his head
with the blanket again.* HALIE *takes a single rose from* DEWIS *and
moves slowly over to* DODGE.) We can't not believe in something. We can't stop believing. We just end up dying if we
stop. Just end up dead. (HALIE *throws the rose gently onto*
DODGE's *blanket. It lands between his knees and stays there.
Long pause as* HALIE *stares at the rose.*)

BRADLEY: Ansel never played basketball.

HALIE: Bradley, I'm warning you. (SHELLY *stands suddenly.*
HALIE *doesn't turn to her but keeps staring at the rose.*)

SHELLY: (*To* HALIE.) Don't you wanna know who I am? Don't you wanna know what I'm doing here?! Standing in the middle of your house. I'm not dead! (SHELLY *crosses toward* HALIE. HALIE *turns slowly to her.*)

HALIE: Did you drink your whiskey?

SHELLY: No! And I'm not going to either!

HALIE: Well, that's a firm stand. It's good to have a firm stand.

SHELLY: I don't have any stand at all. I'm just trying to put all this together. (HALIE *laughs and crosses back to* DEWIS.)

HALIE: (*To* DEWIS.) Surprises, surprises! Did you have any idea we'd be returning to this?

DEWIS: Well, actually—

SHELLY: I came here with your grandson for a little visit! A little, innocent, friendly visit.

HALIE: My grandson?

SHELLY: Yes! That's right. The one no one seems to remember.

HALIE: (*To* DEWIS.) This is getting a little far-fetched.

SHELLY: I told him it was stupid to come back here. To try to pick up from where he left off.

HALIE: Where was that?

SHELLY: Wherever he was when he left here! Six years ago! Ten years ago! Whenever it was! I told him nobody cares. I told him nobody cares anymore. Nobody's going to care.

HALIE: Didn't he listen?

SHELLY: No! No, he didn't. We had to stop off at every tiny little meatball town that he remembered from his boyhood!

HALIE: My grandson?

SHELLY: Every dumb little donut shop he ever kissed a girl in. Every drive-in. Every drag strip. Every football field he ever broke a bone on.

HALIE: (*Suddenly alarmed, to* DODGE.) Where's Tilden?

SHELLY: Don't ignore me! I'm telling you something!

HALIE: Dodge! Where's Tilden gone? (SHELLY *moves violently toward* HALIE.)

SHELLY: (*To* HALIE.) I'm talking to you! I'm standing here talking to you. (BRADLEY *sits up fast on the sofa.* SHELLY *backs away.*)

BRADLEY: (*To* SHELLY.) Don't you yell at my mother!

HALIE: Dodge! (*She kicks* DODGE.) I told you not to let Tilden out of your sight! Where's he gone to?

DODGE: Gimme a drink and I'll tell ya.

DEWIS: Halie, maybe this isn't the right time for a visit. (HALIE *crosses back to* DEWIS.)

HALIE: (*To* DEWIS.) I never should've left! I never, never should've left! Tilden could be anywhere now! Anywhere! He's not in control of his faculties. He wanders. You know how he wanders. Dodge knew that. I told him when I left here. I told him specifically to watch out for Tilden. (BRADLEY *reaches down, grabs* DODGE's *blanket, and yanks it off him. He lays down on the sofa and pulls the blanket over his head.*)

DODGE: He's got my blanket again! He's got my blanket!

HALIE: (*Turning to* BRADLEY.) Bradley! Bradley, put that blanket back! (HALIE *moves toward* BRADLEY. SHELLY *suddenly throws the cup and saucer against the right door.* DEWIS *ducks. The cup and saucer smash into pieces.* HALIE *stops, turns toward* SHELLY. *Everyone freezes.* BRADLEY *slowly pulls his head out from under the blanket, looks toward right door, then to* SHELLY. SHELLY *stares at* HALIE. DEWIS *cowers with the roses.* SHELLY *moves slowly toward* HALIE. *Long pause.* SHELLY *speaks softly.*)

SHELLY: (*To* HALIE.) I am here! I am standing right here in front of you. I am breathing. I am speaking. I am alive! I exist. *DO YOU SEE ME?*

BRADLEY: (*Sitting up on the sofa.*) We don't have to tell you anything, girl. Not a thing. You're not the police are you? You're not the government. You're just some prostitute that Tilden brought in here.

HALIE: Language! I won't have that language in my house! Father, I'm—

SHELLY: (*To* BRADLEY.) You stuck your hand in my mouth and you call me a prostitute! What kind of a weird fucked-up yo-yo are you?

HALIE: Bradley! Did you put your hand in this girl's mouth? You have no idea what kind of diseases she might be carrying.

BRADLEY: I never did. She's lying. She's lying through her teeth.

DEWIS: Halie, I think I'll be running along now. I'll just put the roses in the kitchen. Keep them fresh. A little sugar sometimes helps. (DEWIS *moves toward left.* HALIE *stops him.*)

HALIE: Don't go now, Father! Not now. Please—I'm not sure I can stay afloat.

BRADLEY: I never did anything, Mom! I never touched her! She propositioned me! And I turned her down. I turned her down flat! She's not my type. You know that, Mom. (SHELLY *suddenly grabs her coat off the wooden leg and takes both the leg and coat downstage, away from* BRADLEY.) Mom!

Mom! She's got my leg! She's taken my leg! I never did anything to her! She's stolen my leg! She's a devil, Mom. How did she get in our house? (BRADLEY *reaches pathetically in the air for his leg.* SHELLY *sets it down for a second, puts on her coat fast, and picks up the leg again.* DODGE *starts coughing again softly.*)

HALIE: (*To* SHELLY.) I think we've had about enough of you, young lady. Just about enough. I don't know where you came from or what you're doing here but you're no longer welcome in this house.

SHELLY: (*Laughs, holds the leg.*) No longer welcome!

BRADLEY: Mom! That's my leg! Get my leg back! I can't do anything without my leg! She's trying to torture me. (BRADLEY *keeps on making whimpering sounds and reaching for his leg.*)

HALIE: Give my son back his leg. Right this very minute! Dodge, where did this girl come from? (DODGE *starts laughing softly to himself in between coughs.*)

DODGE: She's a pistol, isn't she?

HALIE: (*To* DEWIS.) Father, do something about this, would you! I'm not about to be terrorized in my own house!

DEWIS: This is out of my domain.

BRADLEY: Gimme back my leg!

HALIE: Oh, shut up, Bradley! Just shut up! You don't need your leg now! Just lay down and shut up! I've never heard such whining. (BRADLEY *whimpers, lies down, and pulls the blanket around him. He keeps one arm outside the blanket, reaching out toward his wooden leg.* DEWIS *cautiously approaches* SHELLY *with the roses in his arms.* SHELLY *clutches the wooden leg to her chest as though she's kidnapped it.*)

DEWIS: (*To* SHELLY.) Now, honestly, dear, wouldn't it be better to talk things out? To try to use some reason? No point in going off the deep end. Nothing to be gained in that.

SHELLY: There isn't any reason here! I can't find a reason for anything.

DEWIS: There's nothing to be afraid of. These are all good people. All righteous souls.

SHELLY: I'm not afraid!

DEWIS: But this is not your house. You have to have some respect.

SHELLY: You're the strangers here, not me.

HALIE: This has gone on far enough!

DEWIS: Halie, please. Let me handle this. I've had some experience.

SHELLY: Don't come near me! Don't anyone come near me. I don't need any words from you. I'm not threatening anybody. I don't even know what I'm doing here. You all say you don't remember Vince, okay, maybe you don't. Maybe it's Vince that's crazy. Maybe he's made this whole family thing up. I don't even care anymore. I was just coming along for the ride. I thought it'd be a nice gesture. Besides, I was curious. He made all of you sound familiar to me. Every one of you. For every name, I had an image. Every time he'd tell me a name, I'd see the person. In fact, each of you was so clear in my mind that I actually believed it was you. I really believed that when I walked through that door that the people who lived here would turn out to be the same people in my imagination. Real people. People with faces. But I don't recognize any of you. Not one. Not even the slightest resemblance.

DEWIS: Well, you can hardly blame others for not fulfilling your hallucination.

SHELLY: It was no hallucination! It was more like a prophecy. You believe in prophecy, don't you, Father?

HALIE: Father, there's no point in talking to her any further. We're just going to have to call the police.

BRADLEY: No! Don't get the police in here. We don't want the police in here. This is our home.

SHELLY: That's right. Bradley's right. Don't you usually settle your affairs in private? Don't you usually take them out in the dark? Out in the back?

BRADLEY: You stay out of our lives! You have no business interfering!

SHELLY: I don't have any business, period. I got nothing to lose. I'm a free agent. (*She moves around, staring at each of them.*)

BRADLEY: You don't know what we've been through. You don't know anything about us!

SHELLY: I know you've got a secret. You've all got a secret. It's so secret, in fact, you're all convinced it never happened. (HALIE *moves to* DEWIS.)

HALIE: Oh, my God, Father! Who is this person?

DODGE: (*Laughing to himself.*) She thinks she's going to get it out of us. She thinks she's going to uncover the truth of the matter. Like a detective or something.

BRADLEY: I'm not telling her anything! Nothing's wrong here! Nothing's ever been wrong! Everything's the way it's supposed to be! Nothing ever happened that's bad. Everything is all right here! We're all good people! We've always been good people. Right from the very start.

DODGE: She thinks she's gonna suddenly bring everything out into the open after all these years.

DEWIS: (*To* SHELLY.) Can't you see that these people want to be left in peace? Don't you have any mercy? They haven't done anything to you.

DODGE: She wants to get to the bottom of it. (*To* SHELLY.) That's it, isn't it? You'd like to get right down to bedrock? Look the beast right dead in the eye. You want me to tell ya? You want me to tell ya what happened? I'll tell ya. I might as well. I wouldn't mind hearing it hit the air after all these years of silence.

BRADLEY: No! Don't listen to him. He doesn't remember anything!

DODGE: I remember the whole thing from start to finish. I remember the day he was born. (*Pause.*)

HALIE: Dodge, if you tell this thing—if you tell this, you'll be dead to me. You'll be just as good as dead.

DODGE: That won't be such a big change, Halie. See this girl, this little girl here, she wants to know. She wants to know something more. And I got this feeling that it doesn't make a bit a difference. I'd sooner tell it to a stranger than anybody else. I'd sooner tell it to the four winds.

BRADLEY: (*To* DODGE.) We made a pact! We made a pact between us! You can't break that now!

DODGE: I don't remember any pact. (*Silence.*) See, we were a well-established family once. Well-established. All the boys were grown. The farm was producing enough milk to fill Lake Michigan twice over. Me and Halie here were pointed toward what looked like the middle part of our life. Everything was settled with us. All we had to do was ride it out. Then Halie got pregnant again. Out the middle a nowhere, she got pregnant. We weren't planning on havin' any more boys. We had enough boys already. In fact, we hadn't been sleepin' in the same bed for about six years.

HALIE: (*Moving toward the stairs.*) I'm not listening to this! I don't have to listen to this!

DODGE: (*Stops* HALIE.) Where are you going?! Upstairs?! You'll just be listenin' to it upstairs! You go outside, you'll be listenin' to it outside. Might as well stay here and listen to it. (HALIE *stays by the stairs. Pause.*) Halie had this kid, see. This baby boy. She had it. I let her have it on her own. All the other boys I had had the best doctors, the best nurses, everything. This one I let her have by herself. This one hurt real bad. Almost killed her, but she had it anyway. It lived, see. It lived. It wanted to grow up in this family. It wanted to be just like us. It wanted to be part of us. It wanted to pretend that I was its father. She wanted me to believe in it. Even when everyone around us knew. Everyone. All our boys knew. Tilden knew.

HALIE: You shut up! Bradley, make him stop!

BRADLEY: I can't.

DODGE: Tilden was the one who knew. Better than any of us. He'd walk for miles with that kid in his arms. Halie let him take it. All night sometimes. He'd walk all night out there in the pasture with it. Talkin' to it. Singin' to it. Used to hear him singing to it. He'd make up stories. He'd tell that kid all kinds a stories. Even when he knew it couldn't understand him. We couldn't let a thing like that continue. We couldn't allow that to grow up right in the middle of our lives. It made everything we'd accomplished look like it was nothin'. Everything was canceled out by this one mistake. This one weakness.

SHELLY: So you . . .

DODGE: I killed it. I drowned it. Just like the runt of a litter. Just drowned it. There was no struggle. No noise. Life just left it. (HALIE *moves toward* BRADLEY.)

HALIE: (*To* BRADLEY.) Ansel would've stopped him! Ansel would've stopped him from telling these lies! He was a hero! A man! A whole man! What's happened to the men in this family?! Where are the men?! (*Suddenly* VINCE *comes crashing through the screen porch door up left, tearing it off its hinges. Everyone but* DODGE *and* BRADLEY *back away from the porch and stare at* VINCE, *who has landed on his stomach on the porch in a drunken stupor. He is singing loudly to himself and hauls himself slowly to his feet. He has a paper shopping bag full of empty booze bottles. He takes them out one at a time as he sings and smashes them at the opposite end of the porch, behind the solid interior door, right.* SHELLY *moves slowly toward right, holding the wooden leg and watching* VINCE.)

VINCE: (*Singing loudly as he hurls bottles.*) "From the halls of Montezuma to the shores of Tripoli. We will fight our country's battles in the air on land and sea." (*He punctuates the words "Montezuma," "Tripoli," "battles," and "sea" with a smashed bottle each. He stops throwing for a second, stares toward right of the porch, shades his eyes with his hand as though looking across to a battlefield, then cups his hands around his mouth and yells across the space of the porch to an imaginary army. The others watch in terror and expectation. To the imagined army.)* Have you had enough over there?! 'Cause there's a lot more here where that came from! (*Pointing to the paper bag full of bottles.*) A helluva lot more! We got enough over here to blow ya from here to Kingdom come! (*He takes another bottle, makes the high whistling sound of a bomb, and throws it toward right porch. Sound of a bottle smashing against a wall. This should be the actual smashing of a bottle and not taped sound. He keeps yelling and heaving bottles one after another.* VINCE *stops for a while, breathing heavily from exhaustion. Long silence as the others watch him.* SHELLY *approaches tentatively in* VINCE's *direction, still holding* BRADLEY's *wooden leg.*)

SHELLY: (*After silence.*) Vince? (VINCE *turns toward her. Peers through the screen.*)

VINCE: Who? What? Vince who? Who's that in there? Is someone in there? (VINCE *pushes his face against the screen from the porch and stares in at everyone.*)

DODGE: Where's my goddamn bottle?!

VINCE: (*Looking in at* DODGE.) What? Who is that? Who's speaking? Whose voice is that?

DODGE: It's me! Your grandfather! Don't play stupid with me! Where's my two bucks!

VINCE: Grandfather? Grandfather? You mean the father of my father? The son of my great-grandfather? That one? When did this start?

DODGE: Where's my bottle?! (HALIE *moves away from* DEWIS, *upstage, peers out at* VINCE, *trying to recognize him.*)

HALIE: Vincent? Is that you, Vincent? (SHELLY *stares at* HALIE, *then looks out at* VINCE.)

VINCE: (*From the porch.*) Vincent who? What is this?! Who are you people?

SHELLY: (*To* HALIE.) Hey, wait a minute. Wait a minute!

HALIE: (*Moving closer to the porch screen.*) We thought you were a murderer or something. Barging in through the door like that.

VINCE: A murderer? No, no, no! How could I be a murderer when I don't exist? A murderer is a living breathing person who takes the life and breath away from another living breathing person. That's a murderer. You've got me mixed up with someone else.

BRADLEY: (*Sitting up on the sofa.*) You get off our front porch, you creep! What're you doing out there breaking bottles? Who are these foreigners anyway! Where did they all come from?

HALIE: (*Moving toward the porch.*) Vincent, what's got into you! Why are you acting like this?

VINCE: Who's that? Who's that speaking?

SHELLY: (*Approaching* HALIE.) You mean you know who he is?

HALIE: Of course I know who he is! That's more than I can say for you, missie.

DODGE: Where's my goddamn bottle? (HALIE *turns back toward* DEWIS *and crosses to him.* VINCE *sings.*)

VINCE: "From the halls of Montezuma to the shores of Tripoli. We will fight our country's battles in the air on land and sea . . ."

HALIE: (*To* DEWIS.) Father, why are you just standing around here when everything's falling apart? Can't you rectify this situation? (DODGE *laughs, coughs.*)

DEWIS: I'm just a guest here, Halie. I don't know what my position is exactly. This is outside my parish anyway. I'm in the quiet part of town.

SHELLY: Vince! Knock it off, will ya! I want to get out of here! This is enough.

VINCE: (*To* SHELLY.) Have they got you prisoner in there, dear? (VINCE *starts to sing again, throwing more bottles as things continue.*)

SHELLY: I'm coming out there, Vince! I'm coming out there and I want us to get in the car and drive away from here.

Anywhere. Just away from here. Far, far away. (SHELLY *moves toward* VINCE's *saxophone case and overcoat. She sets down the wooden leg down left and picks up the saxophone case and overcoat.* VINCE *watches her through the screen.* SHELLY *moves to right door and opens it.*)

VINCE: We'd never make it. We'd drive and we'd drive and we'd drive and we'd never make it. We'd think we were getting farther and farther away. That's what we'd think.

SHELLY: I'm coming out there now, Vince.

VINCE: Don't come out. Don't you dare come out here. It's off-limits. Taboo territory. (VINCE *pulls out a big folding hunting knife and pulls open the blade. He jabs the blade into the screen and starts cutting a hole big enough to climb through.* BRADLEY *cowers in a corner of the sofa as* VINCE *rips open the screen.* DEWIS *takes* HALIE *by the arm and pulls her toward the staircase.*)

DEWIS: Halie, maybe we should go upstairs until this blows over. I'm completely at a loss.

HALIE: I don't understand it. I just don't understand it. He was the sweetest little boy! There was no indication. (DEWIS *drops the roses beside the wooden leg at the foot of the staircase, then escorts* HALIE *quickly up the stairs.* HALIE *keeps looking back at* VINCE *as they climb the stairs.*) There wasn't a mean bone in his body. Everybody loved Vincent. Everyone. He was the perfect baby. So pink and perfect.

DEWIS: He'll be all right after a while. He's just had a few too many, that's all.

HALIE: He used to sing in his sleep. He'd sing. In the middle of the night. The sweetest voice. Like an angel. (*She stops for a moment.*) I used to lie awake listening to it. I used to lie awake thinking it was all right if I died. Because Vincent was an angel. A guardian angel. He'd watch over us. He'd watch over all of us. He would see to it that no harm would come. (DEWIS *takes her all the way up the stairs. They disappear above.* VINCE *is now climbing through the porch screen onto the sofa.* BRADLEY *crashes off the sofa, holding tight to his blanket, keeping it wrapped around him.* SHELLY *is outside on the porch.* VINCE *holds the knife in his teeth once he gets the hole wide enough to climb through.* BRADLEY *starts crawling slowly toward his wooden leg, reaching out for it.*)

DODGE: (*To* VINCE.) Go ahead! Take over the house! Take over the whole goddamn house! You can have it! It's yours! It's been a pain in the neck ever since the very first mortgage. I'm gonna die any second now. Any second. You won't even notice. So I'll settle my affairs once and for all. (*As* DODGE *proclaims his last will and testament,* VINCE *climbs into the room, knife in his mouth, and strides slowly around the space, inspecting his inheritance. He casually notices* BRADLEY *as he crawls toward his leg.* VINCE *moves to the leg and keeps pushing it with his foot so that it's out of* BRADLEY's *reach, then goes on with his inspection. He picks up the roses and carries them around smelling them.* SHELLY *can be seen outside on the porch, moving slowly center and staring in at* VINCE. VINCE *ignores her.*) The house goes to my grandson, Vincent. That's fair and square. All the furnishings, accoutrements, and paraphernalia therein. Everything tacked to the walls or otherwise resting under this roof. My tools—namely my band saw, my skill saw, my drill press, my chain saw, my lathe, my electric sander—all go to my eldest son, Tilden. That is, if he ever shows up again. My Benny Goodman records, my harnesses, my bits, my halters, my brace, my rough rasp, my forge, my welding equipment, my shoeing nails, my levels and bevels, my milking stool—no, not my milking stool—my hammers and chisels and all related materials are to be pushed into a gigantic heap and set ablaze in the very center of my fields. When the blaze is at its highest, preferably on a cold, windless night, my body is to be pitched into the middle of it and burned 'til nothing remains but ash. (*Pause.* VINCE *takes the knife out of his mouth and smells the roses. He's facing toward the audience and doesn't turn around to* SHELLY. *He folds up the knife and pockets it.*)

SHELLY: (*From the porch.*) I'm leaving, Vince. Whether you come or not, I'm leaving. I can't stay here.

VINCE: (*Smelling the roses.*) You'll never make it. You'll see.

SHELLY: (*Moving toward the hole in the screen.*) You're not coming? (VINCE *stays downstage, turns and looks at her.*)

VINCE: I just inherited a house. I've finally been recognized. Didn't you hear?

SHELLY: (*Through the hole, from the porch.*) You want to stay here?

VINCE: (*As he pushes* BRADLEY's *leg out of reach.*) I've gotta carry on the line. It's in the blood. I've gotta see to it that things keep rolling. (BRADLEY *looks up at him from the floor, keeps pulling himself toward his leg.* VINCE *keeps moving it.*)

SHELLY: What happened to you, Vince? You just disappeared. (*Pause.* VINCE *delivers the following speech front.*)

VINCE: I was gonna run last night. I was gonna run and keep right on running. Clear to the Iowa border. I drove all night with the windows open. The old man's two bucks flapping right on the seat beside me. It never stopped raining the whole time. Never stopped once. I could see myself in the windshield. My face. My eyes. I studied my face. Studied everything about it as though I was looking at another man. As though I could see his whole race behind him. Like a mummy's face. I saw him dead and alive at the same time. In the same breath. In the windshield I watched him breathe as though he was frozen in time and every breath marked him. Marked him forever without him knowing. And then his face changed. His face became his father's face. Same bones. Same eyes. Same nose. Same breath. And his father's face changed to his grandfather's face. And it went on like that. Changing. Clear on back to faces I'd never seen before but still recognized. Still recognized the bones underneath. Same eyes. Same mouth. Same breath. I followed my family clear into Iowa. Every last one. Straight into the corn belt and further. Straight back as far as they'd take me. Then it all dissolved. Everything dissolved. Just like that. And that two bucks kept right on flapping on the seat beside me. (SHELLY *stares at him for a while, then reaches through the hole in the screen and sets the saxophone case and* VINCE's *overcoat on the sofa. She looks at* VINCE *again.*)

SHELLY: Bye, Vince. I can't hang around for this. I'm not even related. (*She exits left off the porch.* VINCE *watches her go.* BRADLEY *tries to make a lunge for his wooden leg.* VINCE *quickly picks it up and dangles it over* BRADLEY's *head like a carrot.* BRADLEY *keeps making desperate grabs at the leg.* DEWIS *comes down the staircase and stops halfway, staring at* VINCE *and* BRADLEY. VINCE *looks up at* DEWIS *and smiles. He keeps moving backwards with the leg toward up left as* BRADLEY *crawls after him.*)

VINCE: (*To* DEWIS *as he continues torturing* BRADLEY.) Oh, excuse me, Father. Just getting rid of some of the vermin in the house. This is my house now, ya know? All mine. Everything. Except for the power tools and stuff. I'm gonna get all new equipment anyway. New plows, new tractor, everything. All brand-new. (VINCE *teases* BRADLEY *closer to the up left corner of the stage.*) Start right off on the ground floor. (VINCE *throws* BRADLEY's *wooden leg far offstage left.* BRADLEY *follows his leg offstage, pulling himself along on the ground, whimpering. As* BRADLEY *exits,* VINCE *pulls the blanket off him and throws it over his own shoulder. He crosses toward* DEWIS *with the blanket and smells the roses.* DEWIS *comes to the bottom of the stairs.*)

DEWIS: You'd better go up and see your grandmother. I think you should. It would be the Christian thing.

VINCE: (*Looking upstairs, back to* DEWIS.) My grandmother? There's nobody else in this house. Except for you. And you're leaving, aren't you? (DEWIS *crosses toward right door. He turns back to* VINCE.)

DEWIS: She's going to need someone. I can't help her. I don't know what to do. I don't know what my position is here. I'm quite out of my depths. I'll be the first to admit it. I thought, by now, the Lord would have given me some sign, some guidepost, but I haven't seen it. No sign at all. Just— (VINCE *just stares at him.* DEWIS *goes out the door, crosses the porch and exits left.* VINCE *listens to him leaving. He smells the roses, looks up the staircase, then smells the roses again. He turns and looks upstage at* DODGE. *He crosses up to him and bends over, looking at* DODGE's *open eyes.* DODGE *is dead. His death should have come completely unnoticed.* VINCE *lifts the blanket, then covers* DODGE's *head. He puts* DODGE's *cap on his own head and smells the roses while staring at* DODGE's *body. Long pause.* VINCE *places the roses on* DODGE's *chest, then lays down on the sofa, arms folded behind his head, staring at the ceiling, his body in the same position as* DODGE's. *After a while,* HALIE *is heard coming from above the staircase. The lights start to dim imperceptibly as* HALIE *speaks.* VINCE *keeps staring at the ceiling.*)

HALIE'S VOICE: Dodge? Is that you, Dodge? Tilden was right about the corn, you know. I've never seen such corn. Have you taken a look at it lately? Dazzling. Tall as a man already. This early in the year. Carrots, too. Potatoes. Peas. It's like a paradise out there, Dodge. You oughta take a look. A miracle. I've never seen it like this. Maybe the rain did something. Maybe it was the rain. (*As* HALIE *keeps talking offstage,* TILDEN *appears from left, dripping with mud from the knees down. His arms and hands are covered with mud. In his hands he carries the corpse of a small child at chest level, staring down at it. The corpse mainly consists of bones wrapped in muddy, rotten cloth. He moves slowly downstage toward the staircase, ignoring* VINCE *on the sofa.* VINCE *keeps staring at the ceiling as though* TILDEN *weren't there. As* HALIE *continues,* TILDEN *slowly makes his way up the stairs. His eyes never leave the corpse of the child. The lights keep fading.*) Good hard rain. Takes everything straight down deep to the roots. The rest takes care of itself. You can't force a thing to grow. You can't interfere with it. It's all hidden. Unseen. You just gotta wait 'til it pops up out of the ground. Tiny little shoot. Tiny little white shoot. All hairy and fragile. Strong though. Strong enough to crack the earth even. It's a miracle, Dodge. I've never seen a crop like this in my whole life. Maybe it's the sun. Maybe that's it. Maybe it's the sun. (TILDEN *disappears above. Silence. Lights go to black.*)

END OF PLAY